TO ALASTAIR
THANKS FOR
GIVING ME
MONEY

GU00865762

Never Eat the
Buffet in a
Sex Club*

*Contains no food or sexual references

This is the page that's supposed to have all that legal mumbo jumbo on it. You know, all rights reserved to Aidan Goatley what wrote it.

Seems a waste of a page so here's a poem.

A poem.

My daddy has built a Stargate in his shed.

That's what he says he's done.

Although I don't believe him,

Because I'm 41.

Hello and thanks for making it to page one. This in itself is an achievement. Hopefully if you agree to continue then you'll enjoy what's to follow. This is a collection of things that I've written; some finished, some not, some from my shows and some ideas I think are funny.

I'd like to dedicate this to Brian Andrew Dickson. A man whose humour and spirit inspire others to laugh through the pain that the world sends it's way.

The Joys of Retail

It's the summer of 2006 and I'm in a pool hall in Trowbridge. It is 8:15pm and my companion is taking a shot. He is fidgety and tense as it takes a lot of concentration for him to focus. In between turns he is wandering around the hall looking for cigarette butts he can scrounge to make up a full smoke. My companion is 15 and a child with emotional behavioral difficulties, prone to violence and I am his support worker.

I am terrified of him.

I can't cope with any kind of confrontation but also I can't cope with being broke. The job of support worker is all I could get after getting a 2.2 in scriptwriting from Bournemouth University and finding myself living in the wilds of North Dorset. It's not an easy job and each shift is 24 hours from 10am. With any luck I'll be able to get some sleep tonight providing my companion has a good evening and doesn't let the night terrors get to him. The job can be very confrontational as the young people are heavily traumatized and easy to lash out. Last week one of the other boys pulled a wooden curtain rail from the wall and threatened me with it. I had to stand there with my arms out wide to try and assure him I wasn't a threat to him.

The phone rings. My companion, let's call him Brian, looks up and I can see the concern in his eyes. There are 3 boys in the house that I work in and we work in pairs. A phone call may mean that my work colleague is in trouble with the other two and Brian knows this may stop his evening out.

I look at the phone and it's a friend from Uni phoning.

"It's OK Brian. Personal call."

Brian instantly switches from concerned little boy to put upon teenager as soon as he hears this.

"I'll tell them to phone back later, no problems."

I answer the phone, never taking my eyes from Brian as he is showing signs of agitation now that he does not have my full attention.

"Hiya Aidan it's Gemma!" says Gemma in a voice so loud, bubbly and posh it would be better served being at a Polo event or on the slopes of a Swiss ski resort. She lives in a world I couldn't possibly understand. My favourite conversation with Gemma was when she told me she was distraught because of her hairdresser was very upset.

"Why is she upset?" I asked

""Well she can't fix my hair this week because apparently, Prada don't do ski suits in a size 14. They only go up to 12!"

"Outrageous."

"Like, totally right!"

But back to reality.

"Hi Gemma, listen I'm at work at the moment can I call you back later?"

There is a moment of confusion in Gemma's voice as she tries to comprehend how anyone could possibly be working in the evening.

"Ok lovely but I think daddy is going to phone you in a moment."

This is odd. I have a brief moment to try and work out why her dad would phone me. I've only met him once at his other daughter's wedding. It was a full tuxedo affair held in a castle and I remember feeling massively out of place. I'd hired a suit and was sat amongst a lot of people who had never had to hire clothes in their life. At one point I had gone to the bar, which was all paid for, and arrived at the same time as the aforementioned 'daddy.'

"Thank you for inviting my wife and I."I say trying to sound like I belong in a suit.

"Not at all, not at all" comes the booming response in a voice that sounds like Prince Phillip but with possibly more aggression. Not for the first time I'm glad I don't live in the wild. If I did it would be a short time before my noggin was mounted on this mans wall.

"I was going to buy you a drink but it looks like some idiot's put too much money behind the bar" I say in a desperate attempt to fill the silence.

There is a pause. Mr Crayford (He is the kind of grown up who doesn't have a first name) looks at me in the eyes. There is a steely look, a slight twitch and suddenly a full barrage of laughter.

I start to laugh, concerned that the quip I had made was not that funny and Mr Crayford is about to find a suitable plaque for my head. Instead he just wanders off.

That was 2 years ago.

"I think he's going to offer you a job," says Gemma. Bringing me back from the memory.

With that Gemma hangs up and I am left with the irate Brian and the pool cue that is now being wrung so hard if it needed oxygen it would be dead by now.

"Come on Aid!"

I take my shot and the phone rings again. If I answer the phone again I know Brian will go nuts but I'm intrigued as to what Mr Crayford wants me to do. I've been the support worker at the house for nearly 2 years and I've been terrified for 1 year and 363 days of that time. I'm scared of Brian and he knows it. I reach into my pocket and give him one of my ciggies. This is a major infraction of my job role but I'd rather have 5 minutes peace and suffer the consequences.

"Hello Aidan!" comes the booming voice of Mr Crayford

It transpires that Mr Crayford wants me to be the general manager of his garden centre. It is a squillion sqft, has 32 staff and takes approximately the same amount of money that your average Hollywood superstar gets paid per film, in a year.

I have no retail experience.

I have no management experience.

It is clearly the most ridiculous and stupid thing to have reached my ears.

He wants to pay me £30,000.

I say yes.

A few months later I am stood in an old converted greenhouse. I am wearing a shirt and tie, uncomfortable shoes and have never felt so out of place in my life. I am about to have a crash course in retail management. So far it has lasted 9 years and three companies and 8 branches.

I still have no idea what I'm doing.

What follows is some of the random wonders, horrors and delights of working in the retail sector. I assure you I have only changed the names of everyone else involved under advice from my legal team.

Chapter 2

The horror begins

I'm invited into Mr Crawford's office. I haven't been in it since my 6-hour interview where I extolled the many great ideas I was making up as I went along. The reason is that we're organizing the buying for the Christmas range this year and so I find myself sitting with a group of people I don't know, in the heat of June, deciding which stuff we're going to sell. Next to me is Michael, the former General Manager, Louise, the long-suffering PA to Mr Crayford and Jane, who unbeknown to me was under the impression that she would be the next GM. Naturally she loves me from the start. Especially as word has spread that I'm a friend of the Crayford family.

Along for the day is the poor sales rep who is trying to get past Mr Crayford and his insistence of trying to knock down every price. I have a vested interest as Mr Crayford has promised me a significant 1% bonus if we sell over £1,000,000 during Christmas. Now I'm not as naïve to think that we have a hope in hell to do this but given the right product we may just do it.

Several items go by and the management team says yes or no and debates each item. I don't really join in, as I have no idea what will sell.

"Come on Aidan!" yells Mr Crayford "Get involved!"

Spurred into action I suggest that the next item, a novelty Reindeer that's standing upright with a big belly, is one we should buy. In unison everyone in the room, including the rep, look at me in disbelief.

"Really?" booms Mr Crayford

"Yes. I think he looks fun."

"I think he looks like a Moose!" says Jane.

Everyone agrees and the table starts a debate on if Moose are relevant to Christmas.

"Ok' says Mr Crayford, "We'll have a thousand then!"

And just like that a thousand moose looking reindeer are sold at £3 each. They will sell for £4.99.

Jane looks at me in disgust and Michael leans over.

"Know any Canadians?" he says with his tongue firmly in his cheek.

Flash forward to April the following year and the stock take is happening. Of the thousand Reindeer bought we have about 763 left, which will be in storage till September when the great Moose debate will continue no doubt.

As to my bonus I learnt a valuable lesson during the stock take. Once I had the figure of the Christmas stock left in store and added it to the actual sales the figure came to £750,000. There was no way I could've got that bonus even if we had sold everything. My face must have said everything I was thinking.

I am in the car traveling with Mr Crayford. We are on our way to Birmingham to visit an event called 'Glee.' It's an exhibition of suppliers for garden centers'. Basically where all the buyers go to get the stuff you see in the shops. Mr Crayford is driving his enormous Mercedes as though it is going out of fashion. In the front is Mrs Crayford who likes to come along and have a look. She says very little and just gives the occasional flinch as her husband tries another manoeuvre at warp speed.

I'm sat in the back, feeling like an errant child as Mr Crayford lectures me on garden furniture and how over the 27 years of selling it how he knows better than anyone how to get a good deal from the suppliers.

The only thing that makes the journey bearable is Mr Crawford's reaction to his sat nav. Apparently it came as standard when he bought the car but it is now out of date. The female voice tells him to do things that aren't there roughly every ten minutes, which results in Mr Crayford shouting at the dashboard.

"In 500 yards take the exit onto the A304."

"NO NO NO NO YOU STUPID WOMAN. THERE IS NO EXIT. HOW CAN I TAKE AN EXIT WHEN THERE ISN'T ONE!

Joys of retail #3849409

Day 14.

I fear that my quest is near an end. I have traveled many miles to no avail and it has been days since I last saw any of the guides of this realm. I started the mission with one simple plan, to find the treasure. I do not understand what has gone wrong. I did as I was told by entering the mountain range at the eastern base. Within hours my Sherpa Tallengate and I had found the old

trail and were able to use the Northwest Passage
to traverse the mountains and make it to the
shores of Lake Wakkahinda. The storms that
raged against the aside of our boat were
fearsome. It was as if God himself wanted us to
turn back. Dear Tallengate begged me to turn
back but I made the decision to continue. A
decision that will curse me till the day I die.
Curse me like Tallengate did as we were swept
overboard and he was cast into the murky depths.

I awoke on land. Somehow I had survived but
only long enough to realise the 30-mile trek
through the desert awaited me with nothing but
meager supplies and my own guilt to sustain me.

On and on I went, convinced by the honor of my
mission. On I trekked past sand dune after sand
dune until now. I sit by a rock, a rock as lonely as
my soul. I have failed.

I have no option but to return. I must make my
way back. Back through the desert, across the
great lake, over the mountains and back onto the
shop floor where I can tell that customer;

"Sorry we don't have any left in the warehouse.
We should have some back in next week."

Chapter 2

I am on the roof of Mr Crawford's' garden centre
putting up Christmas lights. The centre does a
roaring trade in Christmas and goes all out on its

displays inside and out. Brandon is showing me where to stand, he's done this many times before and is moaning is the fact that I've made him wear a hi-vis jacket.

"Ain't gonna help me if fall through the roof will it?"

He has a point. We scramble over the roof and attach the lights. Brandon points out which panels to not walk on. As one or two he says a pretty much just for show. Brandon then helps erect and put up the larger display that in on the central roof above the entrance door. It is essentially 2 blue pallets nailed together and then screwed into the roof. On top of that is a 6ft round teak tabletop that is screwed onto the pallets then a metal pole going through the centre tops it. Draping from the top of the pole are lights that spread out like a Maypole. A May pole that could double up as a lightening conductor. Brandon assures me that it will be perfectly safe as this was what was up there for the last four years and if I was really going to worry I should worry about the water that streams in through the guttering when it rains. Water that flows pretty much directly over the light displays downstairs.

"Jesus, how can that be safe?"

"Well when it rains we usually turn off the power to them just in case."

I stand on the roof for a few minutes more wondering how the hell this place hasn't been close down before. When I raise my concerns with Mr Higgins he tells me not to worry. It will all be fine.

One month later and it's a busy Saturday. I'm in the tiling department mopping up rainwater when there is an almighty booming noise from the roof. The noise escalates and water starts streaming down all over. The gutters on the roofs were never designed to be watertight as the contents of greenhouses can usually do with a drop of water. Of course Mr Higgins never spent the money to get them sorted.

I run over to the Christmas section, which is crammed full of customers. There must be at least 200 people in there trashing the place. Water is streaming down the poles and over the lights. There must be at least 50 plugs in here and various extension leads daisy chained to other sockets, half of which are covered in water. I turn to Brendan and while another booming sound comes from above I ask, "Can we just turn it all off?"

Brendan shrugs his shoulders, goes to a plug socket behind him and flicks the switch. Suddenly everything goes off. It was all running from one plug!

There is a moan of disapproval from the crowd, which distracts them for 10 seconds before they go back to trashing the displays. What I presume is thunder rages above me and then I hear a crash shortly followed by my name being called to the front of the store. I run to the tills to find everyone just staring out of the window and as I join them I see that they're not just looking at the rain hammering down. 20ft away in the car park is what's left of what looks like a Volvo S40. The roof and front doors have gone and been replaced by two pallets, a 6ft teak round table top and a metal pole which has lodged into the car and been pushed through the base of the pallets. It looks as though the owner of the car has hastily erected a flagpole.

Thank God the car was empty.

I find the distraught owners and get them a nice cup of tea. I phone Mr Higgins and await the eruption of anger down the phone and boy does he erupt. The owners have asked if we will supply them with a courtesy car. They are both 70 and now car less. Mr Higgins erupts down the phone "WHAT HAVE YOU TOLD THEM AIDAN!"

"I said I'd ask you!"

There is a deathly silence down the phone. I know he's still there as I can hear him breathing.

"It's an act of God." He says and hangs up.

I arrange for a cab to take the poor couple home and assure them that Mr Higgins is dealing with the car situation. 2 days later after much gnashing of teeth a courtesy car is rented out for the couple.

Joys of retail #38307023874

One of the many delights of working for Mr Crayford was his interpretation of employment law. Well not so much his interpretation but his refusal to believe any law had been changed since 1955. One of these was that he would only allow one person to work for a whole year before they qualified for any holiday leave at all. It took me 6 months to convince him otherwise and then he had people who had just been employed on the modern system and all the old staff on what they were used to.

He would also fire people without any process as it was his store and if someone were not performing he would deal with them. This was often spoken in the kind and tone of voice that would indicate the use of exclamation marks.

I often found it equally terrifying and amusing when Mr Crayford lost his temper. He tended to explode and stamp his feet while his face went bright red with anger. It was amusing because Mr Crayford would often be dressed purely in beige. Beige shoes, trousers, shirt, jumper would be his uniform and because he spent half the year in his home in Florida he had a beige perma-tan that would blend in with his outfit. Hence when anger got the better of him it was the only time I could define his face properly.

He tried to get me to fire a trolley boy called Michael. Michael was pretty useless but there is a process that's followed and Mr Crayford was not going to follow it. It also didn't help that the boy was only 17 so he called in the boys' parents, told them their son was not performing and fired him.

One week later and an inevitable claim came in for unfair dismissal. I had the pleasure of informing Mr Crayford over the phone whilst he sat in Miami. There was no escape when he wasn't there and I would have to phone him up every Friday evening and give him the figures for the week. There was no chitchat just a simple 'Good morning' and then 'Monday - £****
against £***** from last year' and so on. If I phoned him at any other time, it would always be bad news. The explosion from the other side of the Atlantic was immense.

A couple of months later and we were sat in the tribunal and their barrister grilled me. As part of the testimony I had to impart ways that Michael had not done his job properly, which included him sneaking off for cigarettes from time to time.

"Would it not be possible Mr Goatley," said the barrister giving it the full Atticus Finch, "That when you say you saw Michael smoking you did, in fact, see another staff member?"

"No."

This guy had really seen too many episodes of LA LAW.

"I put it to you that you did in fact see a staff member called Terry and not Michael who doesn't even smoke."

"Well he does smoke. He may not want to admit it in front of his parents but he does and I certainly did not mistake him for Terry."

"And what make you say that?"

"Well Michael here is 17 and weighs about 75Lbs, Terry is 58 about 220lbs and covered in tattoos."

That was the end of my deposition. The result was that they found in favour of Michael as Mr Crayford had indeed unfairly dismissed him as he lied in his statement the sum awarded was minimal. He was discovered to have lied when one of the magistrates had looked out of the window to see him enjoying a quick smoke with his dad in the smoking area.

Mr Crayford was so delighted with this that he didn't swear once at the lady in the sat-nav.

Joys of retail #87464

I'm sitting in the canteen. Opposite me is a young girl called Karen. I've not really spoken to her much. We're both happily listening to the radio and swapping the occasional bit of chitchat. Karl then enters. Karl is a Canadian guy who is temping at the Garden Centre while at University. He has been over the road to the supermarket to get his lunch.

"Er what's that?" asks Karen

"It's a fish pasta salad." Replies the ever-joyful Karl.

"I hate fish." Says Karen, a look of distaste on her face.

"Really? Are you a vegetarian?" says Karl

"No I just really don't like fish. (PAUSE) I like Tuna though."

That little nugget hangs in the air for a second then Karl takes it up.

"You don't like fish but you like Tuna?"

"Yes." Says Karen oblivious to any problem with that last sentence. "Really can't stand those pilgrims though."

"Pilgrims?"

"Yeah you get them in tins. Pilgrims. They stink."

It takes a few seconds for this to sink in with both Karl and myself as we exchange glances.

"You mean Pilchards?" says Karl

"Nah. Pilgrims. Smell rotten. So you're from Canada right?" adds Karen without drawing breath.

"Yes I am."

"Where is that exactly?"

"You don't know where Canada is?" asks an incredulous Karl

"Nah. Never was any good at geography."

No shit.

"Well it's above America."

"What on top of it!" laughs Karen?

"No. No, not at all. You know like Scotland is above England?"

"Is it?" queries Karen.

Karl is beginning to have a look of desperation. I am staring. This is without doubt the best conversation I have ever witnessed.

"Yeah it is. So Canada is attached to the north of America ok."

"Oh so it's part of America then?"

"The land is but it's a separate country."

"OK." Says Karen.

There seems to be a natural pause in the conversation and Karl takes the opportunity to eat some of his fish pasta salad. Which is a tuna one by the way. Karen on the other hand looks as though she is thinking. I look at Karl and we brace ourselves for the next question.

"So in America right. They have a York and a Birmingham and a Greenwich and a Brighton Beach. Why's that then?" she asks.

"Well" I say "When the Pilchards sailed over there from here…"

SILENCE

Joys of retail #3848459

One of the delights of working in retail has been some of the staff and of all of them the one that stands out was a chap called Paul Barlow. Paul was from Barrow-in-Furness and had lived a life that you would not be ready to believe. He worked in the furniture department of Mr Crayford's garden centre and had the most amazing mop of hair for a man of his age. He was, I think in his early 60's and would always be on time and do a good job with the customers. After a particularly stressful day he approached me and said,

"It's quite tough being in retail management. I remember when I ran a supermarket in Papa New Guinea, boy we had some problems there."

It was this kind of statement that Paul would drop in from time to time that would make him the perfect company. I did try to piece together his life-story as it was as wild and varied as that of a Hollywood film but not quite as believable.

He had started out in the Navy where he had travelled all over the world and ended up working in the south Asia seas. At one point he was hired to sail a ship from Hong Kong to the Philippines but along the way he contracted malaria and fell into a coma miles from anywhere. He drifted close to some islands and was rescued by the local tribe who took him in and saved his life. They had limited contact with the outside world and rarely got any visitors. Paul had a TV in the yacht and with his permission the islanders rigged it up and for half an hour each week turned it on and tried to tune it into something whilst everyone watched in awe at a blur. When Paul had recovered he gave them the TV as a thank you and the island chief attempted to return the favour by donating one of his daughters to accompany him on his journey. Paul graciously declined the offer and made his way to the Philippines where he learnt how to perform as a fire-eater and soon became quite the turn and perform all over the southern hemisphere.

It was while in Hong Kong that he was spotted by a television company and ended up in a gangster show about a casino where he played the head of a rival gang. He didn't speak a word of the language but was given the English version of his lines and then dubbed over. He, in his own words, foolishly turned down the second series as he didn't think it was going anywhere and got a job as an chief engineer on another boat owned by a millionaire. This involved spending a lot of time in Monaco maintaining the boat whilst it sat there empty and unused. Consequently Paul spent a lot of time hanging out with the rich and famous and became very good friends with Elton John who had the boat next to him. Often he would be invited over to a shindig at Elton's.

His contract came to an end and he took up the aforementioned managerial role in Papa New Guinea which had it's own interesting moments. He had to carry a revolver at all times as a tribesman had died from food poisoning and the tribe had blamed the supermarket and decided to take action. He arrived one morning to find the them putting a curse on the store so it and all who worked on it were targets. Whilst there his malaria flared up again and he was forced to return to England where after a short spell in hospital he gained employment with the circus where his fire-breathing act came back into its forte. Of course this didn't all come out at once. It would be drip fed to me in gentle conversations, none of which were contrived for my benefit. For example a Chinese woman came in once and Paul was able to converse with her in Cantonese. Another time an elderly Asian man came up to the desk and was mumbling incoherently. It was only Paul "Hang on, I learnt Urdu back in 87," who was able to decipher that the man was a diabetic and in need of sugar.

It was an amazing story and one that at times I thought may be slightly embellished for dramatic effect but one day Paul arrived at work carrying a couple of videotapes. Apparently he had been sitting in a café in Worthing one afternoon when a Chinese guy approached him looking amazed to see him there.

The chap remembered him from the show in Hong Kong and it turned out was a massive fan. Some negotiation later and the chap got a copy for Paul and so that morning we stopped recoding the CCTV and watched our Paul in a scene jumping out of a car to put a stop to a gang shooting amongst the title sequence for this show. The other tape was from Papa New Guinea and showed tribesmen performing the cursing ritual on the store; Paul was stood to one side smoking a cigarette.

It was all true. The last I saw of Paul he was living in Arundel and delighted to have regained contact with his now grown up children.

JOINING PET-R-US

Joys of retail #2949404

I had recently joined a major chain of pet stores when I got an invitation to attend something called 'commercial training' which was to be hosted by the Operations director. I have already heard his name mentioned in hushed tones so I know it's important that I attend the event, which is being held in the North roughly 250 miles away. I get an email saying which hotel they'll put me into. I check Google maps and the hotel appears to be a good 45 mins from head office so I factor this into my journey plan.

I don't have a sat-nav. I've never have had one and am quite happy to look at a map and get by with road signs and a keen sense of direction. We have lovely road signs. They have their own font. It's called Transport 1.I set off the day before; find the hotel and try and sleep. The next morning I awake early, put my suit on and leave the hotel at 7:30am. According to the route planner it should only take me 45 minutes to get to head office and I'd rather sit in my car for 20 minutes and turn up appearing fresh.

Disaster! The journey with traffic takes me an hour and a half and I arrive bang on 9am when the meeting is due to start. I dump the car in the nearest spot and race into the reception area where there is no one to be seen. I look at my watch it is now 9:03am and I've missed the start. With any luck they'll do a bit of chitchat and the boss man will add on another couple of minutes for any latecomers.

I ask at reception.

"Training? There's no training here love."

"But I had an email. The address was for here."

"Yes the email was sent from here but the training is at the NDC."

I have no idea what the NDC is and luckily the look on my face tells the receptionist that fact.

"The National Distribution Centre?" she says.

"Where is the national distribution thingy then?"

"Did you stay at the Travelodge next to the stadium?"

"Yes I did."

"Well it's two minutes from there, here's the address you can put it into your sat-nav love."

"I do not have a sat-nav" I declare and race out of the building.

Oh crap I'm an hour and a half away from my first meeting with my bosses, bosses, boss. I jump in my car and begin to drive so fast I can only hope I travel back in time. I get to the bloody NDC, go to the security gate and of course have the delight of explaining my story to the guards.

"You should get a sat-nav mate."

"I don't need a sat-nav. According to the information I was given I made it to where I thought this meeting was."

I'm shepparded along to the training room. I'm sweaty, disheveled and nervous. I am now an hour and a half late. I enter the room and have to explain to everyone why I'm late and once again someone (undoubtedly an acolyte type) states that I should get a sat-nav. I am about to kill him when the Operations Director tells everyone to settle down so they can carry on.

"Come on now, let's get this done as soon as possible. As you know I could've been in Sweden today but instead I'm here." He says alluding to some information that I had missed out on.

Sat Nav boy pipes up "Oh I'm sure we wouldn't have minded going to Sweden for this Sir" in a tone designed to convey arse kissing of the highest order.

My brain frazzled from the 3 hours of driving and nervous tension shuts down temporarily and my stupid big mouth opens up.

"Sweden. Christ, imagine how fucking late I would've been then?"

Joys of retail #3959505.4

Often managerial retail types will refer to a piece of store set up as "good theatre.' As in it gives a show to customers.
I can't tell you how hard it is when I hear that not to shout,
"Theatre! Theatre! You know nothing. I studied Ibsen at the Schweargen conservatory of the performing arts!"

And flounce off.

Joys of retail #0883930

I am at a managers meeting. The area manager is holding court. This one is a large guy. Barrel chested and from Kent. Sat at the top of the table he is surrounded by his acolytes. In any regional group there are always at least 1 or 2 managers who want to curry favour with the big alpha boss. All Area managers are 'alphas.' The effect is as if the last supper had taken place at a KFC

The meeting starts and the area manager has something secretive to tell us. We know this because he speaks in hushed tones and looks around himself just in case any interloper is listening in furtively, despite there being nothing but wall behind him.

"Ere. Listen up. Word has it that the boss will be making an appearance today. So look sharp and behave."

Oh god. The last time we met this guy he had decided that his team should be known as 'retail marines.' This according to him was a battle and we should all be on the front fighting for sales.

I hate him. He is a cock.

Then as if on cue, he appears at the rear of the room.

"Morning marines!" he shouts.

The acolytes shout morning back. I nod a hello in his direction.

"I'm starting with prizes today!"

He then produces from his bag a cup. It is a white standard mug and on it is emblazoned 'RETAIL MARINE! WELL DONE!'

I want him to die horribly.

The mug is handed to one of the acolytes and we are told to pass it along so we can all get a good look at the legend emblazoned on its side.

"Now that gentlemen is your trophy of honour. The manager of the month will get one. Carry on."

Joys of retail #6573930

I am at a work conference being held at Alton Towers. The evening event is about to happen and it is fancy dress. I hate fancy dress. My daughter loves to dress up and I love my daughter but I won't even do fancy dress at home so why should I do it with 450 pet store managers that I don't know.

The theme is pirates. Our area manager had spread word that everyone must attend and wear an outfit. He also had told us the week before that Matalan had fancy dress costumes so there would be no excuse. I stand in my hotel room wearing my outfit. At the shop there were 2 choices of pirate outfit, a Johnny Depp Pirates of the Caribbean one or a more old fashioned 1950s

Stewart Granger style. I opt for the later. I look like a twat. I feel like a twat.

The day has been spent cramming 20 minutes of information into 4 hours of presentations. We then had to go on a team building exercise. This involved walking around the park and going on every ride. I hate theme parks. Nothing makes me more nauseous than the thought of hurtling round a track in a cart that has been built and maintained by a succession of bored employees on minimum wage. Plus they make me feel ill.

My plan is to go downstairs, endure the meal, listen to the speeches and escape as quickly as possible. I walk down to the main room to see that virtually everyone has gone for the Johnny Depp outfit.

"Why are you dressed like a cavalier?" asks everyone I meet.

"I'm Stewart... oh forget it"

There is a table plan and I am sat next to my area manager. A man so volumous he has garnered the nickname '1985.' I ask why and apparently that was the last time he saw his penis.

Oh how I laughed.

I want to go home. Opposite me is another newbie to the team. He is sat quite still and is covered in grey sheets and what looks like a mast sticking out of his head.

"I'm a ghost ship."

This is the extent of the evening's conversation.

Joys of retail #94749303

"Aidan you need to be tougher. Give em some agro give em shit!"

I can't really; well that's not my style sir.

"Why not?"

"Well I guess cos I'm fundamentally a Buddhist sir."

"BUDDHIST BUDDHIST?!?!?! Aidan, there is no space for Buddhism in retail!"

Joys of retail #384

Work has supplied us with new t-shirts to promote healthy food for pets. They are black and on the front in bold white it says 'ASK ME ABOUT NUTRITION.'

I put mine on and it fits but it is a bit snug around my large belly. I vow to wear it permanently at work and see if anyone else spots the irony.

Joys of retail #655758

I am walking around with a new Area Manager. Unlike the last one it becomes apparent that this one knows the facts and figures.

"So which department is your strongest?"

Er I um

"It's dog food. What's your staff turnover rate?"

Well I have er the well…

"It's 22.3%"

Gosh that's… well… a figure.

"Tell me Aidan, did this bumbling Hugh Grant impression work on my predecessor?"

Gosh. Well he never asked any questions.

Joys of retail #03939

"OH MY GOD!" says my deputy manager as she runs into the office in a state more exuberant than has ever been displayed before.

"KATIE PRICE IS IN THE STORE!"

She runs out again. I have at that point no real idea who she is talking about but a quick Google and it transpires that she is the former model known as 'Jordan' and now a television reality star and 'novelist.'

I come out on to the shop floor to see what the fuss is about. My deputy comes back to me; "She's buying stuff for her dogs. Can I go on the till?"

It has taken the arrival of a celebrity to get her on the till but who am I to complain. I nod and she dashes off to the tills.

I notice outside the main doors is a bright pink Range Rover. It looks horrendous. It belongs to the aforementioned literary genius in my store.

A queue develops so I jump onto another till to help clear it and Katie Price comes to my side of the till chatting to the friend she is with. She is tiny and orange. She is so orange she actually clashes with the colour of her own car. I start to scan the items, a dog bed and a few collars when my deputy (completely ignoring her queue) steps at my side.

"I see you've gone for a bed from our new range?" she says butting in to the conversation "Lovely aren't they?"

Katie Price looks over to my deputy and with a tone of voice that expresses disgust says,

"Don't matter does it? It'll soon be covered in shit."

And with that the most orange woman in the world leaves and drives away. It is as though the sun is setting in the distance.

Joys of retail #48494030

One thing I have noticed in retail is the willing destruction of the English language. Don't get me wrong I'm not a grammar Nazi, I couldn't tell you the right place to put a comma but I'd at least like it to make sense.

Recently there has been a trend in restaurants putting out signs that say 'SERVED INSIDE, AUTHENTIC STREET FOOD." I'm not usually one to quibble but surely once 'street food' is made and served inside it is no longer 'street food' but just 'food.'

In one store I worked in they used to sell cat litter trays that came in large, giant and extra giant! What the hell size cat needs and extra giant cat litter tray?! That's not a cat, that's a leopard. And if you need a cat tray that large may I suggest you probably have to let the cat go where it wants.

At Pets they had a treat for Chinchillas that encouraged them to chew and therefore protect their teeth. This was sold by having a picture of a chinchilla with a speech bubble saying 'I want a natural Hollywood smile.' I remember spending ages once trying to explain my contempt for this to a marketing executive. My complaint that a) why would a chinchilla want super white teeth and b) there is nothing natural about Hollywood fell on deaf ears. "It's just a bit of fun Aidan?"

Another thing that's always annoyed me is the selling of 'Wild' bird food. Apart from the fact that feeding wild animals destroys their natural feeding patterns the very fact that they are wild means that they should technically be able to fend for themselves. Also why spend money to encourage an animal to poo in your garden? Do you need poo in your garden? If so give me a call and I'll come and poo in your garden for you.

"Oh I say what a lovely collection of poo. Do you use wild bird food?"

"No we pay a nice boy to do it for us. He's very good."

You can actually buy 'no mess' wild bird food that doesn't produce excess waste.

People are starving in the world and this is what money is spent on.

Joys of retail #12234

The store looks perfect as the team await the arrival of the area manager. We haven't seen him here in 3 months and the last time he came there was lots tutting and disappointment from him on how we were doing. We've just done a few late nights to make sure our visit goes well.

He was supposed to be here at 9:30am. It is now 2pm.

He enters the store.

"Fuck me Aid. That was a hell of a journey. You put the kettle on I'm away for a shit."

He makes straight for the staff area so I go to the kitchen and make him a coffee.

10 minutes later he emerges.

"Woah Fucking 'ell Aid I wouldn't go in there for a while. Listen I got to get to Worthing. Place looks great. See you soon."

With that he is gone.

Joys of retail #393938

At a managers meeting.

One of the acolytes is strongly agreeing with the area manager. This means either no one is listening or he's really done badly on his sales figures. I confess that I stopped listening ages ago and my sales figures are bad. I'm just not very good at meetings and usually drift off halfway through as retail jargon blends into one long monotonous drawl of acronyms.

"How are your KPI's and the effect on your CTS, which in turn will stop your WFM performing from your LFL?"

I have no idea what is being said. I'm getting ready to nod at the right moment. I've worked out that at some point the area manager will interrupt the acolyte and say something like this.

"Look it's not difficult is it gentlemen? We're all retailers here…" and then he'll give us a veiled threat about our jobs that could also double as a master-class in passive-aggression. Nothing hurts me more than when we all get called retailers. I'm not a retailer. Like most of my colleagues I ended up here.

I'm keeping an eye on Stuart from the Hasledean store. He's a good solid middle of the table store guy. As soon as he nods I'll nod too aaaaaaaaaaaaaaaaaaaaaaaaaaaaaaaaaaaaaaaaaaaaaan d there's the nod!

I nod.

Joys of retail #875.4

It is amazing how often customers say the same thing again and again. At Pets-R-Us it was always at the till. People would often get embarrassed at the amount of money they would spend on their pets so when they get to that bit at the till when they found out how much it would often cause stunned silence. Without fail they would always give the same response,

"The pets eat better than I do!" and then give a laugh at their originality.

The temptation to respond "Really? May I recommend a dietician?" Always came forefront in my mind.

Also when you checked the bank notes for forgeries.

"Printed it myself this morning!"

"Really sir? Could you wait there while I call the police?"

Joys of retail #6765656

I'm at the Nottingham university centre. It's another conference and my head is spinning. The company has decided that this year's theme will be 'Stars in their Eyes' and be a talent contest. Each region is supposed to produce a champion (read 'sucker') to go up and do a bit for the team. This is supposed to be like the TV show of the same name and the champions dressed like their chosen heroes will basically do karaoke.

This message got jumbled up and my area manager has just asked me to do some stand up for 5 minutes instead. I'm standing backstage with, amongst others, a couple dressed like John

Travolta and Olivia Newton John and a chap in full KISS make up. I am wearing a plain t-shirt, green combats and my leather jacket. When asked what my costume is I tell them I'm the Christopher Ecclestone Doctor Who. They look at me blankly.

Out front are 500 pet store managers, everyone from head office, the board of directors and representatives of the hedge fund company that have just bought us.

Word has spread that I'll be doing stand up and I've had a mixture of looks ranging from positive to 'oh my God what is he going to say' from the Operations director, Sarah. A woman who seemingly has the looks of Joanna Lumley combined with the charm and grace of Theresa May.

"Don't do anything stupid Mr Goatley." Says Sarah as though rehearsing to be Bond Villain. Normally I would've taken this very seriously but she is currently wearing Day-Glo track gear and has an inflatable banana under her arm. I have no idea who she is supposed to be.

A Yorkshire version of Adam Ant finishes warbling on stage and I am called up. At this point in my comedy career I haven't performed to an audience this large.

"Hello to you all. I'd like to welcome you all, especially the representatives of Madeupname who are here with us today. You guys should know that Sarah was worried I would say something stupid to offend you up here."

The room suddenly empties of oxygen as the entire company management waits for one of their colleagues to commit career suicide.

"But it's OK Sarah. I rang the bank and they told me the cheque has cleared. I could say anything right now!"

599 people erupt in laughter, probably more out of relief than anything else. Sarah does not.

I do the rest of my 5 minutes and get a big round of applause. Mostly because during my set I'd picked on the loss prevention team and at one point called the head of the department 'Gandalf' as when it comes to audit 'NONE SHALL PASS!'

I come offstage and let the KISS guy have his turn. A chap comes up, he is the owner of the hedge fund. He's worth about 3 billion and is dressed like Angus Young of AC/DC. He says something, I presume it's positive as he's smiling and shaking my hand. I can't hear a word as 'God Gave Rock n Roll to You' is blasting out of a speaker.

"I hate you and this company." I mouth back.

He does a fake laugh, pretending to have heard, then walks back to his table.

I make towards a table at the back and sit down next to 'Gandalf.'

"Prick." He says.

Joys of retail #2348

Mid-November in the pet store in Horsham. Horsham is quite a nice area and we rarely have any trouble. Most customers are elderly country types. Everything is looking shiny, as we've just had our fish tanks re-fitted.

An older lady walks around, she is the only person in the store. As she makes her exit I say hello, but she is clearly quite deaf.

"HELLO" I try again.

"HELLO" she booms back, "I DO NOT BUY ANYTHING HERE BUT I DO LIKE TO HAVE A GOOD LOOK AROUND!"

"THANK YOU MADAM. DID YOU SEE THE NEW FISH TANKS?"

The lady stops dead in her tracks and gives me a steely-eyed stare.

"TANKS! TANKS? WHY WOULD I WANT ANY TANKS? I HAVE TWO LAKES!"

She storms off angrily.

2 days later I receive an email from customer services. Apparently a lady felt rudely insulted by the pushy sales staff.

Joys of retail #2348b

Mid-July in the pet store in Worthing. Worthing is, well it should be, a lovely place but for some reason there is an overriding sense of anger. A woman approaches me brandishing some scissors.

"YOU OUGHT TO BE ASHAMED! YOU OUGHT TO BE ASHAMED OF YOURSELVES!" she screams across the shop floor.

"YOU LEFT THESE SCISSORS ON THE SIDE OVER THERE. A YOUNG CHILD COULD HAVE PICKED THESE UP..."

At this point I am in total agreement with what she is saying.

""THEY COULD HAVE PICKED THESE SCISSORS UP... AND STABBED YOU IN THE BACK WITH THEM!"

Welcome to Worthing.

Joys of retail #2348c

I arrive at the Newhaven store. I've never been to Newhaven before. It's an old ferry port that seems a little run down. There's not much there apart from the ferry and a small retail park. I'm chatting to a colleague and trying to be positive.

"So what's in Newhaven?" I ask in possibly my most positive voice.

"Poverty." She replies.

Two days later I have to send her home for coming in still a little drunk from her night out. I was first suspicious when she wrapped a black jumper around her head and leapt out at colleagues shouting, "I'M A NINJA!

Joys of retail #

One of the problems of selling pets is that everyone thinks that they know what's best for the animals themselves. Some people think that they shouldn't be sold at all, that pet stores are evil places and will protest at every available point. Usually while coming in to buy the pet food that they need for their pets.

There are also the customers who want to buy every pet they possibly could get into their house and we called them bunny-huggers. At Pets-R-Us we were trained to look out for both kinds but also for a third, our own staff. The problem being that staff would often adapt the regulations and rules laid down by the company and interpret them to their own benefit. They would decline animal sales, as they would make snap judgements on people coming into the store. We also were not allowed to reserve animals as this can lead to problems with customers and staff getting confused and angry.

A classic example of this was when on a Monday morning a manager discovered that 2 separate families were promised 2 particular rabbits on the Saturday just gone. The problem was that another member of staff altogether had sold them both on the Sunday. So the manager does the logical thing and chooses to phone the 1st family and tell them that the rabbit is unavailable.

Unfortunately he doesn't tell them the truth and instead decides to tell them that the rabbit had sadly died, that it was very sudden and tragic and that it hardly ever happens. The family were upset but understood and they would come in next weekend and see the manager personally about a new rabbit.

He then phones the second family and once again decides to tell them that the rabbit had sadly died, that it was very sudden and tragic and that it hardly ever happens.

This is where the problem snowballs. Unbeknownst to the manager the two families are not only friends but also neighbours and also in the SAME room when the phone calls were made. As they've just been told that both animals have died that looked perfectly healthy not two days beforehand they make the decision to phone the RSPCA and warn them that something isn't right in the state of Denmark. Within hours the RSPCA have visited the store, head office have been informed, an area manager and the companies own animal inspector have visited and the manager of the store is then suspended and eventually loses his job.

My own career with the company became somewhat difficult when I developed an allergy to dust and fur. This would lead to some interesting moments when someone wanted a pet.

"I'll just get a colleague to help."

"Can't you do it?" the customers would ask.

"No, sadly I've developed an allergy to fur" I would say awaiting the inevitable response.

"Bit silly working here then eh?"

I would often have to stem my frustration at their collective misunderstanding of the word 'developed.'

"No it's since I started working here. It's not that I wanted a challenge."

Joys of retail #2038484

I'm in Nottingham again for yet another conference. As I sit here in my room I feel like Captain Willard at the beginning of Apocalypse Now waiting for another mission. There's another fancy dress theme but I've long since stopped caring what it was. Not right now though as there appears to be a party going on next door. This is not unusual at work conferences, as people seem to behave as though it is the biggest night of their lives. Dear God we have to sit through 8 hours of tedium tomorrow and then have the inappropriately named 'gala' dinner, why won't they go to sleep.

I try to control my anger but I lose it when Sandra returns.

I have no idea who Sandra is, was or will be but at 1:30am I know that she has returned from wherever the hell she has been.

"SANDRA!" "SANDRA." "WHERE HAVE YOU BEEN SANDRA?" comes the cry of people as they rejoice at the return of their ever-popular comrade. For a full 10 minutes.

"SANDRA WHERE HAVE YOU BEEN SANDRA? SANDRA? SANDRA? SANDRA?"

With that last call I explode. I throw open my door to see several people in the corridor just drinking and dancing, all the other doors are open as this appears to be the party corridor. Calls of 'Sandra' can still be heard from inside the next room. I walk to the door way and obviously my look of total anger silences them all in seconds.

"Which one is Sandra?" I ask. All remain silent.

"Well in that case my I also express my delight at her return. HOWEVER I would suggest that by the fact that for the last 15 minutes I have heard nothing but questions for the aforementioned 'Sandra' that she has not actually answered ONCE, THAT SHE IS SO DRUNK THAT SHE DOES NOT KNOW WHERE SHE HAS BEEN OR FOR THAT MATTER THAT SHE HAS RETURNED OR PROBABLY WHO THE FUCK SHE IS! WOULD YOU PLEASE THEREFORE KINDLY SHUT THE FUCK UP ABOUT SANDRA AND LET SOME OF US SLEEP!"

There is a stony silence as I realise that I may have gone too far but I try to style it out by giving everyone the stare hoping that no one will start a fight, as I'm not capable of dealing with that. It is then that I notice that in the corner of the room is my area manager. The bully himself. I wilt inside and want the world to swallow me up. I turn to walk away and as I do so I hear my boss say "Well, I guess he doesn't like Sandra then!" and everyone laughs.

The party carries on and they make a conscious effort to be even louder. We're on the ground floor so I collect my blanket and jacket and climb out of the window. I walk away from the building and the sound of the party carries across the quiet night as though their constant taunts about Sandra follow me. I get to my car and arrange the front seat so I can sleep in it and eventually I drift off.

I wake up achy at 5:30am and return to my room, which is now in silence. The corridor is strewn with empty cans and drink bottles. The open doors of last night now closed as the offenders sleep off their alcohol. I shower and dress and exit my room and walk along the corridor opening all the hallway doors and wedging them open with the fire extinguishers. I then return to the furthest point from where I want to be and brace myself against the wall. I give a count of three, launch myself down the corridor and arms outstretched bang on every door as I run along. "FIRE! FIRE! FIRE!" I shout. I get to the corner and throw myself around it then slow down and walk towards the central reception area. Within a minute I am on the far side of the building in the canteen getting a nice cup of coffee. When the alarm goes off for real I smile, pick up my coffee and make my way outside to join my 'team.'

Fuck you Sandra. Fuck you.

Joys of retail #3938474

It's 9pm on a Sunday evening and I'm at a stock take at the Worthing branch of Pets-R-Us. We've finished the initial count so pizza and fizzy drinks have been brought round. The manager of this store is worriedly walking around with the stock supervisor and waiting for what will come up in the second count. I'm standing on the shop floor and can overhear a conversation that 2 other managers are having. Around us are several colleagues just sitting around, who being bored senseless are also listening in.

The two managers are described as 'driven,' because this is the polite way of saying 'Nazi.' One of them, Michael is known as being a bit creepy. This is due to always sitting at the top of the table at meetings and offering to do every job the area manager asks to be done and because during one drunken evening he, whilst naked, tried to get into the bed of his roommate at conference. This repulsion of him is not due to any homophobic reason but purely the thought of Michael being naked would make anyone shudder. The other was known as 'Dr Evil.' This was due to his alopecia rendering him completely hairless and being an utter bastard.

"Well if you need to deal with it you need to deal with it." Says Michael "Get em out of your building and fire the fuckers."

Dr Evil nods in full agreement.

"Yeah it's like I said, you can't stand the heat get out of the kitchen. We're all for the carrot but they always need the stick too!"

I can't help but wonder at how inappropriate this conversation is and how it's being held in earshot of colleagues. "Aidan?" Oh God. I have no wish to be dragged into their Alpha pissing contest.

"Aidan, how do you control your team?" asks Dr Evil.

"Easy. Any trouble from my team and it's an instant loss of drinks at cocktail hour!"

"What?" they both ask in unison.

"Oh yes. You'd be surprised how effective the loss of a banana daiquiri can do to a colleague when it comes to team meetings around the piano!"

Their eyes are blinking as though trying to compute what is being said.

"Piano?"

"Yes, Piano. Have one in the warehouse. Got it all set up so we gave team meetings and sing song around it. Good for morale. Daiquiris are a house speciality. You should come next Wednesday, we're having a Gershwin night." I say and make my exit from the floor.

The looks on their faces still trying to work out what I said whilst the colleagues were suppressing giggles will stay with me forever.

Several months go by and word has spread that I have a piano in my warehouse. I get an email from someone at head office telling me it is illegal to have alcohol on the premises. I assure him that the daiquiris are served 'virgin' style and he has nothing to worry about. It is only when the Operations Director visits me a few months later when I realise that this rumour has reached the top of the business.

"You don't really have a piano here do you Aidan?"

Joys of retail #0001 Plants R Us

I have just written this letter. Should I send it?

Dear *****

I am writing to inform you of
my intention to resign. Under my contract I am
giving 4 weeks notice.

I need those 4 weeks to apply for my visa to go to
Bogotá.

Bogotá is the capital of Colombia and
Cundinamarca Department, with a population of
8,854,722 in 2015. Bogotá and its metropolitan
area had a population of over 13 million in 2015.
Bogotá is the fastest growing major city in Latin
America, and is expected to have around 25
million inhabitants by 2038.

It is with that expansion that I intend to form my
own improvised interpretive dance company. It is
my dream.

Interpretive dance describes a family of modern
dance styles commencing in its formative years,
around 1900, with Isadora Duncan. It used
classical concert music but marked a departure
from traditional concert dance. It seeks to
translate human emotions, conditions, situations
or fantasies into movement and dramatic
expression, or else adapts traditional ethnic
movements into more modern expressions.

I cannot wait.

It is going to be wild. Dance is my life.

Regards

Aidan Eduardo Fernandez Goatley

Joys of retail #9394032 Brightview Garden
Centre Group

"The problem is your brim!"

My brim sir?

"Yes the brim. It's too wide!"

Right. Sorry sir could you possibly clarify what
you mean by brim?

"THE BRIM! I've told you IT'S TOO WIDE!"

Yes sir you've said that. It's just which brim you
mean sir?

"Oh didn't I say?"

No sir.

"Your teacups. Brim's too wide, makes the tea

cool down too quickly. You'll sort it out won't you?"

Joys of retail #294949 Brightview Garden Centre Group

Due to the inconceivable fact that for some reason I'm not on at the Apollo or being offered publishing deals for my books, I find today I am wearing a suit.

I have a second interview at 11 for a new job.

The bonus of this is it is still in retail so at least the 'Joys of Retail' book can get more material.

Wish me luck.

Joys of retail #039493"3

"Hi Aidan I thought you might
Like to
Know how you did at your assessment?"

Yeah. Of course*

*no just cut to the chase

10 minutes of waffle later

"So we'd like to ask you to come to a second interview."

Oh thank god**

**OH THANK FUCK

Joys of retail #304049383

Assessment interview day.

This company seem nice. They have a structure that seems to work.

Plus the gluten free rolls at lunch were divine.

Joys of retail #294959595

7:30am

An area manager is in a store with 2 managers. He has arrived in his brand new company car. A BMW 3 series. Black.

AM: I want this changed. The wall is in the wrong place. It all needs to move 6ft to the left. You'll need to rebuild it. I'll be back on Thursday with my boss. It better be done.

ME: Who with?

*There then follows an extensive conversation where the AM can't grasp the concept that there are no staff available as they are all pissed off. Manager 2 steps in with a question to change the subject.

MANAGER 2: So how's the new company car?

AM: Disappointing. I ordered it with to have a burnt oak leather interior but instead it's more a burgundy. Gutted. All my fellow BMW owners are laughing at me.

*Conversation ends as I burst out laughing

Uncontrollably.

M1: Sorry. I drive a Chevrolet. It's grey.

Joys of retail #92738494

"Oh shit. It's only October take it down mate!'

Well it's nearly November?

"Fuck off prick.

Joys of retail #78965

"The problem I have is watching you lot laughing!"

Why, is that a problem?

"Well it proves you're not working!"

Er well we were having a chat about our work plan for the week.

"I demand to speak to the manager!"

I am the manager madam.

"But but you're wearing shorts!"

I was laughing too madam and yet they say men can't multi-task.

"Oh piss off"

Joys of retail #39474930.4

I have staff member called Mary. She is quite a timid, mouse like girl in her mid 30's. She has been off ill for a few weeks so I check up on her return that she is ok. I need to do a 'return to work' interview as I have a duty of care to make sure she is ok.

I ask her if we can do this and she looks terrified. I try to explain but she scampers off to work in the plant section. A couple of days go by and I notice that her mum and dad have been dropping her off and staying in the restaurant till her shifts have finished.

I approach them both.

"Hi. Sorry to disturb but I'm wondering if I can have a quick word about Mary?"

The mum looks terrified.

"She's not in any trouble. I can just see she's not in top form and I want to make sure she's ok."

"Ok. I'd best let you know." She replies in a tone that is best described as mysterious.

I sit down. The father says nothing to me, doesn't even look me in the eye, and just looks straight ahead.

"It's important that you know that, well, Mary is not possessed. She has what is known as an 'attachment.'

I try my hardest to assimilate what this woman has just said to me.

"An attachment?"

"Yes a lost soul has attached itself to Mary and we're seeing a specialist to get it removed."

My mind races as it tries to comprehend what it is being told.

"A specialist, a doctor?"

The mum then explains that they are spiritualists and they have engaged the services of a professional medium to help remove the attachment.

"So you're telling me that your daughter has a lost soul attached to her and you've been seeing a medium to get it removed?"

"Yes. It's actually very common."

I try my hardest not to laugh. They clearly believe but my concern is that Mary and possibly her parents need to see a medical professional. The chap they are seeing (I've looked at his website charges £85 a session and can even do it over Skype) is helping they say.

"Don't you think it might be an idea to see a medical doctor?" I venture.

"Why what can they do? I mean how can a GP stop a spirit from punching her from the inside?"

I don't know what to do.

"Ok. Is Mary ok though? Will she be ok to work?"

"Yes she's working really hard to get this under control."

"Good. Ok." I say thinking I need to someone at head office immediately.

"Of course we have to tie her down at night."

SILENCE.

I stare at the mum. Then at the dad.

The dad turns and looks at me, tears in his eyes, he says nothing.

"OK. Well... er... like I said I just wanted to check she was ok."

I leave them. What the hell just happened and how am I going to relay this to someone in HR?

Joys of retail ☐#949494b☐

I find one of the best ways to get to sleep is to try and count how many times at work I've been asked "Excuse me. Do you work here?"

I've always found this amazing, as I'm 6ft3, 18stone and wear a uniform of an XL luminous lime green t-shirt with purple trim. On the front it has the name of the company and on the back it carries the legend - "How can I help you?"

This is a wonderful design flaw as people will only see the offer of help as it walks away.

I usually answer every fifth time with - "No I don't but do you see that guy over there in the luminous lime green t-shirt? He does."

Scenes of Retail #436

"Hi, You won't claim to remember me but about every month you come in here. Load up a basket and then walk around eyeing the staff long enough to decide when the right chance to leave without paying. Most times you go for the 'sudden' phone call when approached and claim to have to leave suddenly or not have brought your purse. Usually with far too much acting involved. I don't want to be rude but you'll never get into Rada with performances like that.
So All I'm saying is that today can you just admit defeat and leave? You'll never win any acting awards and I'm just tired. You can try and steal from me another day if you like?"

Blank face.

"Fair enough."

Shoplifter departs.

Joys of retail #2848595

I'm on the tills a woman approaches.

That's a very fresh baby there.

"Yes she is only 2 and a half weeks old. Sorry she's screaming she's very hungry. I'll feed her when I get to the car"

Oh you can feed her here if you like. Just leave the stuff here. I'll jump on another till.

"Oh should I go in the bathroom?"

You don't have to. You can use the restaurant or the loos are over there. Wherever you feel comfortable.

The woman leaves her purse and goods. She returns with her now quiet child a few minutes later.

"Thanks."

No worries. Congratulations by the way.

"Thanks."

She leaves. A happy customer.

Joys of retail. #2949505

There is no joy today. 16th day on a row.

My days start at 8, finish at 6. No real breaks. So that's 160 hours I've just done in 2 weeks. 80hour weeks.

My contract states 39.

Last night my boss said he'd be in my store at 7:30am. He expected me to be here. I informed him that I couldn't be in that early as I have to drop the child to her football practice on Friday mornings at 7:45.

There was a pause as he expected me to apologise.

I am trapped by the money.

I actually have the weekend off. Which is amazing. I don't even want to think about work but I will spend the time looking for another job.

I am also doing a charity gig tomorrow night for Grace Eyre who look after people with learning difficulties. It's at the Purple Playhouse in Brighton. Come along support the cause and give me a hug too if you can.

Love

Aid x

ps more regular Joys of Retail will return as soon
as come out of hiding in the loos

Joys of retail #4563

"Hi Aidan. Do you know if you're going back to
the ****** store or staying at the ***** store?"

I don't know. Why?

"HR have been in the phone and asked if I was
aware that a new Manager was starting but I don't
know where."

Oh. Well do they know?

"No."

Right. Well who hired him?

"I don't know."

So you're asking if I know where I'm going, so
you can work out where this guy is going so you
can tell HR to tell him because they don't know,
but no one actually knows where he is going?

"Yes."

Shall we just ask him then? Maybe he knows. What's his name?

"I don't know."

So a guy we know nothing about is apparently starting with us to run a store and we don't know which store or when?

"Yes"

Joys of retail #46783

"I shouldn't be telling you this but..."

*looks around to check coast is clear

"Next week is Conifer week. 3 for 2"

Wow.

"Keep it a schtum."

Joys of retail #98652

So you're saying that I'm 'too nice'

"Yes Aidan. It's all very well to promise to do your best; you've got to be the best. No-one wakes up and goes to work to come 3rd do they?"

But surely if we create a positive atmosphere or "be nice" as you say then surely that would permeate to the staff. Who in turn would be positive to the customers who in turn would respond by spending more money?

"It's a lofty ideal Aidan but it doesn't work in real life. You've got to be tougher. That's why people like Jeremy Corbyn won't push the button. You have to have the drive to do what's right."

So what you're saying is that in order for me to succeed here I need to use the threat of nuclear war and not be like Jeremy Corbyn?

"Yes."

So I'm the Jeremy Corbyn of retail?

PAUSE.

"Let's look at yesterday's sales figures."

Joys of retail #347585

TEAM MEETING

BOSS: So a bit of an icebreaker. If you could be

invisible for a day what would you do? Keep it clean! (Last bit said with knowing wink)

MANAGER 1: "I'd actually like to go to my store and see what happens without me there."

MANAGER 2: "I'd like to go to Ipswich Town FC and see what really happens there behind the scenes."

*Several managers later

ME: I'd like to find somewhere quiet and read my book. It sounds peaceful no one being able to bother you.

BOSS............. Ok. So, sales figures!

Joys of retail #67854

Colleague enters office.

"I've put a holiday request in for 14th December."

Sorry but you know no one is allowed off during December. It's our busiest time.

"Well my daughters coming from Australia so I'll be off anyway."

So you put in the request because..?

"Well I'll be off anyway."

Colleague leaves.

Joys of retail #356798

"Hi I am here to do your stock take. My name is Brian."

Hi I'm Aidan.

"Ok Andy."

Joys of retail #23030

"Hi this is Gayle from head office. I'm trying to track down all the vehicles in the business. Do you have any there?

"Yes. There's an Audi A5 Quattro, white convertible TDI that's been sitting in the car park for 8 months. Dumped here by a manager who left ages ago. I'm really please you're calling actually as my team here are a bit upset seeing it every day just rusting away while cutbacks are going on."

"Ah I'm calling about Vans. Do you have a van there?"

"Yes a white van registration G57676F."

"Oh. You have that one, I'd had that down at another centre."

"Right. What about the Audi?"

"Oh someone else will have to call you up about that. I don't know who but someone will."

The Audi sits there for another 4 months.

Joys of retail #666

I'm at a managers meeting with another new Area manager. This one is hilarious as he is using every single type of management speak. I've already started logging down his favourites. In reverse order we have;

3/ 'Let's just box this one off.' – 4 times in 3 hours

2/ 'That's a great piece of theatre' – 5 times in 3 hours

1/ 'Let's throw that one out with the bathwater' – 8 times!

He also has the bonus of sounding like a radio DJ. Any second I expect him to break for Julie with the traffic report but instead he announces that there's an important announcement from head office to go through.

Apparently we have to give out 'availability' sheets to all out staff.

"Are we cutting their hours then?

"No."

"Really?"

"No but don't tell them that."

"The company have decided to ensure customers have more staff during peak hours so they're going to make the staff more flexible by scheduling a base rota to keep the stores running at their quietest. We will then offer the staff the opportunity to 'flex up' during busy periods. Effectively they won't be losing too much."

There is a stony silence.

"Just one question," I ask trying not to sound like Columbo. "If I have a colleague on say, 32 hours, and after this process he is down to 12 hours when we're not busy. Am I supposed to expect him to happily accept this and say no worries when do you want me? I'll be lynched. These people have mortgages and bills dependent on the wages they get now."

"Well it's only a possibility."

"Really"

"No" but don't tell them that yet.

More silence in the room.

"That's fucked," I say

I look directly at the area manager "I know." He says.

Within 3 months he will have left the company. It takes a further 6 for me to do the same. We both started on the same day.

Joys of retail #39404

I walk round to the toilets where I'm told a customer wants to complain.

"Hello sir what seems to be the problem?"

"Your disabled loo is locked. I want to use it."

I check that the door has its red tab showing.

"Someone's in there sir. I'm sure they won't be long or you can use the gents over there."

"Well how long will they be?"

"I don't know sir."

"Why not?" he responds quite aggressively.

"I have no idea sir. I don't check customers' bowel movements when they come in sir"

"I NEED THE LOO!" he screams at me then grabs hold of my collar. "I need to empty my bag" he whispers.

Ah.

At that point the door opens and an older lady emerges and the man rushes past her.

"Must av ad the fish" says the old dear as she gives me a wink.

Joys of retail #030304

Derek, my new determined and driven area manager is trying to understand why we are behind on the tasks needed to be done. We look at the rota and then at the tasks. Then at the rota again.

"Well I have no problem with you guys doing some late nights." He says as though that's the answer.

""Well I have no problem apart from no-one will do extra hours during the day and certainly not during the evenings."

He stares at me blankly. I know this is not without purpose. This is the point where I'm supposed to say it'll be ok and get everything sorted. I say nothing.

"Well you'll have to get people in for extra shifts during the days then."

I take a quick breath as I recall that I covered that problem the last time I opened my mouth.

"OK. Who?"

His eyes flash with incredulity "Well you're the one that gets paid the big bucks Aidan" he says as if that's the answer I need.

"But surely you get paid bigger bucks than I?" blurts out of my mouth.

He has no answer and just stares at me.

EPILOGUE

Joys of retail #Final

It's November 2015 and I'm sitting in the office of the garden centre I've been running. It's a Thursday. On Monday I handed in my notice to escape this place. I haven't heard from any of the grown ups.

I look up to notice that Rob, the regional director has just walked in. He sits down and utters the words "We need to have a chat…"

Ooops. This doesn't sound good. It turns out that some of the 'Joys of retail' have been leaked and the big bosses have decreed that I must go.

"You are aware that I handed in my notice on Monday." I ask.

"Yes. So why don't we have say a gentleman's agreement. We will pay you for the remainder of your notice on the understanding that you no longer post anything on Facebook whilst you are technically still employed by us. Also we'd like you to delete the posts."

"They're not all about this place."

"Yes but you're in the public eye."

I try to stifle a laugh at this statement. My last gig before this was to 6 people of which only 2 I didn't know.

"As such you could bring the company into disrepute so I must ask you to leave."

"Fair enough." I say.

I hand over my keys (only after I wish I'd handed over my badge too like in a cop movie) and make for the day.

"Is it true you're writing a book?" He asks.

"Yes."

"May I suggest that you tread carefully? From a legal standpoint."

"Mmmm What you mean change the names of the companies and the people involved and make sure that I emphasize that certain events may have been changed for dramatic effect and therefore it's an entire work of fiction?"

"Yes."

"I'll think about it."

A Dubai Diary

In 2015 I was lucky to be asked to perform in Dubai. It meant that I would be away for three days on a whistle stop visit. I wrote this while there.

Hi, my name is Aidan and I'm trying to be a comedian.

I say 'trying' because no one really tells you when you are one and some people will even argue about that. At the time of writing I've been 'doing' comedy for 5 years, seriously for about four.

Many comics will think that 5 years makes you a proper comic. Others if you are getting paid and don't have to do anything else to pay the rent.

That's the problem with comedy. There's no union.

I'm 43 and have a wife and child. The child flatly refuses to work, which is quite disappointing to say the least, so I have a full time job as the manager of a pet store. I have a degree in Scriptwriting so I'm perfectly qualified to do absolutely nothing.

I always wanted to be a stand-up. When I was a kid instead of rocking out with my tennis racket I would be lip-synching to Billy Connolly and Richard Pryor. I remember once, aged 14, reciting almost word for word Billy Connolly's 'An Audience with' to a girl at a party and trying to impress her. She laughed all the way through then snogged the guy who'd been drinking all-night and trying to fight the smaller kids. I couldn't get up on a stage though. The thought of public speaking would scare the crap out of me.

When I was at university I was asked to compere a charity night. They had organised for 2 proper comedians to do their acts and didn't have a budget for a third. I foolishly agreed and wrote some material especially.

I was awful. I shook, stuttered and crawled my way through the opening. During the break, my stomach tied in knots, I sat in a toilet cubicle and heard the following exchange.

"What do you think?"

"Bloody funny."

"Yeah but that guy with the beard is shit!"

I checked but couldn't escape through the toilet so I had to go out and start the second half. I apologised profusely for being shit and brought on the second act.

It wasn't until 10 years later that under the persuasion of my wife and my good friend Bill Gleave that I gave it another go.

My first actual gig was on 4th August 2009 to mild indifference in a small pub and I loved it.

In 2011 I did my first ever Edinburgh Fringe show and it was a fantastic experience. If you've always wanted to go then make sure you don't miss it next year. To me it's a slice of heaven.

Edinburgh is one of the most beautiful cities in the world. Steeped in history and with architectural beauty at each turn makes it a visual delight. The fact that its excellent inhabitants endure the world's biggest arts festival every August is testament to their tolerance and welcoming nature. That and their ability to avoid the Royal Mile.

The fringe was always a goal and to have my own show there, a dream.

My show '10 films with my Dad' did quite well in its first year. . The show is about how my dad and I didn't talk much as I grew up and how we tended to watch a lot of films. I had good audiences and a couple of nice reviews including a lovely one from The Scotsman on the final day. Armed with this review I decided to bring it back the next year and from there it has just built and built. In 2014 it had its 150th performance and was playing daily in the 140-seat ballroom of The Voodoo Rooms on West Register Street. (*It's now 2018 and it's still going*)

I couldn't have been happier with its success. I had performed it in a few other places around the UK but outside of the Fringe I wasn't really getting many bookings as a 'straight' stand up. So I was incredibly surprised to be offered the opportunity to perform the show as part of the first Dubai laughing Comedy Festival in December of 2014.

Ray, the booker, had seen the show whilst in Edinburgh and along with his business partner was prepared to pay for me to come out and perform.

What follows is a diary, of sorts, of my visit. The combination of jet lag, confusion and to be honest, complete bafflement as to my being there led my mind to wander whilst during my visit. Hence there are stories in this that will take you where my mind was going.

I can only apologise.

Day 1

Wednesday 17th December

Evening. I'm currently writing this sitting at the
back of a big empty bar. They are playing Rizzle
Kicks. I could've stayed in Brighton for the
same experience.

I'm here to do my show and it would seem that
comedy venues are the same the world over. One
nervous promoter drinking already and saying
'I'm just here for the jokes myself' and one very
calm tech guy who methodically will nod at the
promoter randomly to indicate that he should
chill and everything will be just fine.

Lovely.

I am not complaining. It is important that you
know that. I am very lucky.

My flight was at 5pm yesterday. I'm terrified of
flying and would not be doing this normally. I've
got an aisle seat and am perched next to 2 Aussie
guys who look around 18. I let them know if I
fall asleep and they need the loo just to give me a
nudge and I'll shift. They say 'cheers' and that is
the extent of our conversation. Within seconds
headphones appear and they are selecting what

films to watch on the little TV screens in front of them.

I try and calm my nerves by flicking through the selection of films available but nothing screams out at me. The only thing screaming is my mind.

"GET OFF THE PLANE! GET OFF THE PLANE! ARE YOU MAD? THESE THINGS GO DOWN, THESE THINGS GO DOWN!"

So with that calming influence in the background I select 'Godzilla.' I get to the end of the credits and the films stops and instead a prayer is played on the screens in Arabic but with English subtitles.

The Arabic language seems quite pleasant and as I'm about to face certain doom at 39,000ft the words sound soothing. The same can be said of the safety demonstration, which is done first in Arabic. I decide there and then that as we head earthbound to our doom I will only listen to the Arabic version of 'BRACE FOR IMPACT' as I'm sure it will be calming.

Godzilla is a dull film. I was looking forward to watching it but it takes an hour for the big guy to show up and when he does we cut to news footage watched on a small television. I last another 10 minutes and switch over to 'Dawn of the Planet of the Apes.' The miniscule screen and engine noise does little to help me distinguish what the hell is going on. I switch to 'Expendables 3' and for some reason I am transfixed by its awfulness.

As far as I can tell, a secret group of mercenaries called the expendables, who all have massive tattoos saying 'Expendable' on their arms despite being secret, travel around in a plane grunting a lot. The plane is also emblazoned with their logo (Secret groups always think a lot about marketing) and they travel to a generic African country where their mission (I have no idea what their mission was. Between Stallone's grunting and explosions it was lost in translation) goes badly wrong and one of their team is hurt.

He's not dead though and given he's part of a team called 'Expendables' you'd expect them to, well, expect some losses. All this does is make the cast go from grunting to doing a lot of staring into camera. At one point Stallone stares into the camera for so long you can almost sense the shopping list he is reciting in his head.

Soon after, more explosions occur and naturally more grunting. Then just when you think it can't get any worse, Hollywood's favourite anti-Semite Mel Gibson turns up and looks angry. I get the feeling he probably looks angry most of the time but I figure that if his belief system is correct, God will forgive him. The subtitles are in Arabic, so as a bonus I now know how to grunt in Farsi.

We land at 4:30am this morning and after a slight delay am collected by the promoter, Ray, in his little Kia. Its microscopic size is in perfect relation to the seat I have just spent 7 hours sitting in while watching bad movies and eating airplane food. The food actually was quite good. It was Chicken Tikka.

It's bloody lovely to see Ray. Although after I've been on a plane it's bloody lovely to see anyone. The airport is ridiculously busy and people are running around left right and centre.

Ray's driving is incredibly scary. I felt safer on the plane.

He launches into his tales of setting up with the venues while simultaneously checking the map function on his phone and looking in every direction bar the one in front. It's like being in a bumper car but with commentary.

After taking a corner far too fast I comment on his driving and how it's a bit frightening.

"Everyone says that," says Ray with a slight hurt tone to his voice.

"Well, I'm not one to jump on a bandwagon, Ray but surely if everyone says that…"

"But everyone's wrong." Says Ray with a level of self-confidence I only wish I could muster.

We somehow make it to the hotel. There is of course some argument over which room I'm supposed to be in but eventually at 6am I get into bed. I would've got to sleep earlier but I don't feel comfortable for 2 reasons. Firstly it's not my bed. My wife, child and 2 dogs that regularly attack my sleeping body during the night are not here. . I'm used to sleeping on roughly 2 inches of mattress with little or no duvet. Consequently my mind, faced with the possibility of actually getting REM sleep, panics.

The second reason is the price of the diet cokes here. I had glanced at the room service menu when I arrived and realised that the price of two cokes is equivalent to the national debt of a small country or a steak dinner. Seriously the soup is £20.

Eventually I sleep.

The phone buzzes loudly in my ear at 11:30.

I have a visitor. It's my friend Nev. I went to University with Nev and he is one of the loveliest men in existence. He's a journalist and film critic and has been over for the Dubai Film Festival. He currently writes for Empire Film Magazine, an achievement he has never crowed about. I remember one week I had been moaning about my pet store job and how I had spent a week clearing out guinea pig poo. He had just got back from L.A. where he had lunch with Jack Nicholson in Jack Nicholson's house. It was difficult not to hate him a little for that. Although he once admitted to wearing a vest the day he had to interview Bruce Willis so he's impossible to hate.

He has an hour before his plane so we meet in the lobby restaurant and have a diet coke each. I have a steak salad. I'm feeling extravagant.

We chat about the 7 years since we last met. The irony of coming half way round the world when we are usually in the same country is not lost on my sleep-deprived brain. I ask him about Dubai and he tells me he's spent most of his time in various screenings so he hasn't really had time to see much of it.

Too soon he is away in a cab and I wonder when and where we'll meet again.

Mad Dogs and Englishmen go out in the mid-day sun and I am hit by a wave of heat the moment I step outside. I proudly wave away offers of taxi cabs and stride purposefully down the road in my shorts and t-shirt. The hotel is in the Bur Dubai part of town, which I later learnt is known as the dark-side. So called due to its notoriety during the summer months when the heat becomes unbearable and ex-pats send their wives and children away for a couple of months. As a result they all head to this part of town for bar crawls and epic drinking sessions but at midday there is relative peace in the daytime heat. I head down the road and pass a building site to me right. On my left is a highway and only some non-descript buildings on the other side. I make it as far as the corner and several taxi cabs beep to gain my attention. Why would I be walking? Suddenly and without any provocation my nose decides to bleed quite profusely and so a great exploration is called to an end and I return to the hotel.

I spend the afternoon snoozing and watching a terrible film with Bruce Willis and Henry Cavill in it called 'The Cold Light of Day.' It was one of those ones that has a good set up and then gradually descends into tedium. (Rather like Bruce Willis) Sigourney Weaver is in it too. She looks so bored. So very, very bored. There's one good bit when the car she has just crashed slides down some stairs. Bruce has the good fortune to be shot early on in proceedings but the camera keeps going back to him giving the impression that he'll suddenly wake up and kick ass. He doesn't of course as he's clearly in this film for the pay cheque and the free trip to Spain where it's set. Henry Cavill spends the rest of the time looking constipated and in desperate need of a hug. During the course of the film which is set over a 24 hour period he is shot, stabbed, beaten up and in 3 separate car crashes. No wonder he became Superman.

I end up at the gig venue, which tonight is in a room below the hotel. It's called 'The Music Room' and is bloody enormous. It could easily hold 400 which is way too big for comedy if only a small audience show up. The night is not being run by Ray and I've been given this gig as a sort of warm up by some other promoters. There's a band on beforehand (always worrying) which consists of a young singer and a drummer and backing track. I get chatting to the drummer who is called Graham. He lives out here and is on top form banter wise. We conclude that Phil Collins is the unifying force in the world. It's true. Trust me, if you get a group of people together and play the middle verse of 'In the Air Tonight' I guarantee that within seconds they'll all be preparing to do the big drum break.

DADA DADA DADA DADA DUMM DUMM AND I CAN FEEL IT…. etc

Amazingly an audience arrives and we do the show to a truly multinational crowd. English, Arab and Indian. It goes well. Through nerves I forget a few bits and then re-work them in later. I edit as I go realising that the show has several references that may fall flat to a foreign audience. One joke uses the cheap supermarket 'Lidl' as its punch line. It falls horribly flat so I talk to a chap called Raoul in the front row. I explain to him (and indirectly to the audience) that the gag didn't work as it was a local reference. Raoul suggests that I substitute a shop called 'Lulu' which is a big cheap supermarket here. At this point everyone else in the audience agrees that would be best and we pretty much workshop the gag together. I think I got away with it.

The evening is topped off when I discover the hotel has me down as full board! I'm only here for one more night so I reward myself with a steak, Greek salad, Calamari and a cool glass of water.

I get back to my room and await slumber which arrives the moment my head touches the pillow. I dream of Henry Cavill who apologises for looking distressed while looking distressed.

Dubai Diary Day 2.

"There's these people and they're trapped in a house. It's getting hotter and hotter and then it turns out it's a dolls house?"

The benefit of being a super geek is people often set you challenges and my hostess, trying to find the answer to an old memory, set this one.

My day started with a rapid visit to the breakfast room. Dear Lord what a spread. There was the usual buffet selection along with several curry options! This is the kind of move western civilisation has been missing, curry for breakfast. I realise of course that leftover curry has often been consumed at this time of day but this option would make even a Travelodge tolerable.

My plate is soon loaded with hash browns, beans, mushrooms, curry, and turkey sausages. The lack of bacon is due to this being a Muslim country. But over on the opposite side of the restaurant is a table with a serving tray. The label says 'PORK STATION.'

This is epic civilisation. Bacon and Curry! I open the lid to discover the biggest amount of bacon I have ever seen in my life. I love bacon.

I'm off to do a radio interview today on a local radio station. Ray (the promoter) was going to pick me up but I get the message to get a cab. Which is a good thing as I don't think Ray's driving will help my nerves today. I'm soon poured into the back of a rather lovely Lexus. I know it's a Lexus because the hotel staff keep telling me it's a Lexus.

"Mr Goatley, the Lexus will take you to your destination."

"Mr Goatley, there is a Lexus waiting for you outside."

I half expect to be told of a finance deal for Lexus available for me.

My destination is Media City. Everything in Dubai is separated into 'city' sections. There's a Sports City, a Motor City, an Internet City etc. Media city is where all the radio stations and TV stuff is going on.

My driver guides me through the centre of Dubai, which is, odd. It's odd because there is a desert and then there is the most amazing collection of high-rise buildings slapped around. It's a surreal experience. It's like a very hot Milton Keynes. With sand.

I do the radio show which is tremendous fun.

I have a free afternoon and end up at the Dubai Mall. It is enormous. 3 floors of consumerist heaven. I go to the food court and am instantly overwhelmed by the choice and walk around 5 times without being able to choose. Bizarrely the only section empty is the Ice Cream Bar?!?! I fail to understand how in temperatures of 30 degrees the shops can sell jackets but an ice cream bar is empty. I don't go in as my paranoia kicks in. I must be wrong and the other avoiding customers must be right. I settle for Chinese and am sat on a table next to an Ice Rink.

"I thought it might be cooler for you here sir?" says the waitress.

I want to hug her but am distracted by a woman in a Hijab speeding past on her skates. The Black material flying behind her. I can't see her face but there must be a massive smile on it.

I plug into the wifi and get a message from Laurence, a friend I have known since primary school and with whom I'll be staying for the remainder of my stay. The best way to describe Laurence is that his favourite James Bond was Roger Moore and he has styled himself on the man for years. He's waiting for me in another Mall.

There are many Malls in Dubai. Roughly 52 per person. You could spend a week in each and never run out of shops to visit.

I make for the Metro. I always feel the best way to get to know a city is to take its public transport and this system is clean. Seriously clean. Spotless. I buy a ticket in regular class and am soon surrounded by people from every nation. I mean every non-white nation. I'm in Nigel Farage's worst nightmare and it's lovely. Dubai is a place where people come to work and are accepted no matter the culture. Around me are Indians, Pakistani's, Malaysians, Arabs and probably a few more I couldn't tell. I know there is far more to the way people and workers are treated here but on this Metro train is just a world travelling in peace.

I get to the Ibn Battuta Mall. Ibn Battuta was the Arabian Marco Polo. A great traveller and consequently the mall is separated into different country sections. I plonk myself down in an Ottoman designed Starbucks (don't ask) and wait for Laurence. When I first met him Laurence had been living in Dubai and as an 8 year old he would remind us of this on an hourly basis.

When he arrives Laurence has clearly had an upgrade because this finely suited man resembles Pierce Brosnan now. He looks amazing. Seriously his suit is immaculate. Dubai is obviously doing him a lot of good. I don't tell him this of course. We are blokes after all.

"Fuck, you look like shit." I say.

Soon I am at his house where I meet his wife Amelie and his two beautiful children, Madeline and Juliette. I had received a tip off that the girls love Doctor Who and my present of a couple of Dr Who annuals go down a storm. I am upgraded to honorary uncle and am sat down in their garden for a BBQ dinner.

It would be very easy to be jealous of Laurence's life as I sit in his garden as wild parrots fly from tree to tree. I am instantly overcome with pride for my friend.

The kids go to bed and Amelie asks me about that doll's house show she saw once when she was young. It scared the crap out of her and she's never forgotten it. After a brief bit of Aidan searching I find out it's an old Hammer House of Mystery and Suspense called 'Child's Play.' We settle down to watch it on Youtube. It is bloody awful. You can never go back.

Dubai Diary Day 3

I wake up only semi-aware of where I am. For some reason the memory of seeing a building that says 'Scottish Dental Centre' on the side pops into my head and I remember I'm at my friend Laurance Langdon's house in Dubai.

Team Langdon are already up and I can hear them up and running. Today we're off to the desert so we pile into the car and head out into the open. Soon I'm surrounded by great swathes of land either side of the road. Next to the road is a cycle path. Apparently one of the rulers of Dubai was driving along when he spotted people cycling out in the desert so he had an 80km cycle path built alongside the main road.

I cannot believe that anyone would want to use this but soon I see a series of spandex covered fools peddling away and even some people jogging! Really?!

I respond to this as any right minded British gentleman abroad should by turning up the air-conditioning and feeling exhausted.

A few side turnings later and we arrive at the edge of the sand dunes. Laurance lowers the air pressure in the tires and warns me, "Don't panic but I'll have to move at some speed to make sure we don't get stuck in the sand."

I am about to express my worries when the youngest of Team Langdon (Juliette 4 3/4) interrupts with a 'WEEEEEEEEEEEEEEEEEEEEEEEEEEEEEEE EEEEEEEEEEEEEE'

2 minutes and a lot of up and down later (I am such a wuss) we arrive in a clearing and to total silence.

It's an amazing feeling and I soon realise I've been walking around with a mad grin on my face all day. The kids start to body board down the sand dunes and I act like the most British person ever and put up an umbrella. I get sunstroke under a 60w bulb so the fact I'm out here is a miracle. Without really realising it I've started to laugh. Laurance's wife, Amelie, asks what's so funny.

"I'm in the desert." I reply to a look that may be wondering if I have sunstroke already.

Laurance has a plan though and he's decided we're going to re-create the first shot from the new Star Wars Awakens trailer. He picks a spot and pushes record on my iphone camera. I wait a few seconds, pop up from below, open my umbrella and walk off. Later when I edit it to the sound from the trailer it makes a killer gag. In fact if nothing else happens on this trip the fact we shot something in the desert makes me smile even more.

We have a picnic in the dunes and head back to the city.

I have 2 gigs tonight. The first is at Q Underground, a venue underneath the Holiday Inn Al Barsha. I'm a bit nervous because Laurance and Amelie are coming and they're bringing friends. As a comic there's nothing worse than friends coming to see you. The 'what if I'm shit' factor plays heavy and I fear they'll pat me on the shoulder in a way that indicates that it's never too late to try accountancy.

What makes it worse is that they've brought friends with them. Now my brain is panicking as not only will my friends be disappointed with a wasted evening but I'll have ruined the friendship they had with their guests! This is how my brain works.

We get to the venue and there is a poster of me and another comic in the lobby. Now I feel really nervous and incredibly self-conscious. It's about the 167th time I've done this show but I still get nervous every time. Will there be an audience, will there be a microphone, and will there be laughs.

It goes rather well. The audience are well up for it and they join in and it works. Phew.

I say goodbye to the audience and dash out of the door for my second gig which is on the other side of the city, in the financial district.

Ray, Laurance and I jump into a cab and we race across town. I'm in a post gig high and a pre gig low. This results in me grinning like a loon but only inwardly.

The night is called The Real Flava Comedy Club and I've been told it's inhabited by the very rich 'Cool club' crowd. I am also opening for a female American Muslim comic. I have never felt so out of place. I'm sure the MC, a 'DJ Bliss' (I shit you not) will introduce me as cannon fodder but instead I hear "Opening tonight we have an international comic…"

I look around looking to see who this will be before I slowly realise he's talking about me. I hear my name and go on.

In the front row is a hugely muscled dude in a white t-shirt called Mo. I ask him what he does?

"I'm a pimp." He replies in a voice that implies that he really is and that I should back off.

"Of course you are darling." I reply and the crowd thankfully laughs.

The gig goes really well. A mixture of material and mockery goes down well. I get paid and we make our exit.

On the way back I ask the guys about the Scottish Dental Centre which turns out to be real and not a bizarre hallucination.

"So what is that all about then?"

"It's just Dubai man." Says Laurance. "It's just Dubai."

Dubai Diary day 4

My adrenalin rush from last night's gigs lasted till 3am, so I'm very pleased to be up at 8am. I get up anyway thinking that Team Langdon will be awake and I'll have an excuse to watch kids' cartoons with the girls but there is no sign of life. Eventually the girls come down and the eldest, Madeline (8), is staging a protest. She doesn't want to visit the Souk today and isn't happy about it one little bit. I swiftly calculate that by using bribery I will assist in this slight upset in the plans. I do this by suggesting that I was thinking of buying ice creams while we were out.

Juliet nods happily at this thought but Madeline escalates the protest.

What sets this apart from other child protests is that she's created a placard that read's 'Still NO!' and she walks around the kitchen and living room in silent protest. It is one of the funniest things I've seen. Shortly after some supreme negotiating skills by her parents (threats, violence begging etc) we pile into the car and head over to the old town.

The Souk is the old market and is everything you'd expect from an Arabian shopping experience. Stall and shop owners step out and politely ask where you're from. Curse them and their trap of politeness. Soon I am drawn into a conversation with a gentleman about Brighton and pashminas. Although I suspect he may be faking his interest in my home town as once I've declared I do not wish to buy a garment his interest in Brighton & Hove Albion's rough patch disappears.

Laurance guides us down a side alley and suddenly we are at a riverside restaurant. Boats of all shapes and sizes cruise past as I sit there in the shade. The smell of diesel oil occasionally wafts over and I am taken back to times spent with my dad on boats around the world. It's amazing how smells can transport you back to earlier events.

My Arabic grill arrives, a selection of meats and what looks like a small bird grilled and placed on top. We try to work out what it is. It's a either a small mutant chicken or a quail. The arrival of a live pigeon on the guard-rail to my left ensures that whatever animal it may be, it will never be eaten. My hypocrisy in being a carnivore only goes so far.

We jump on a water taxi and for the price of 1 Dirham each we get a trip across the river. We're with locals and tourists alike and our battered little taxi chugs away happily. I realise I'm never more happy than on the water. My youth was spent on boats with my dad and as the sun shines off the river I'm reminded how when she was younger I used to tell my daughter that the light was diamonds hidden in the sea.

We get to the old town and walk through the different sections of the Souk. There is the spice area, fabrics and at the end of our brief tour the Gold Souk. A lane with nothing but jewelry shops and offers of fake Rolex's. It's like walking into the junk mail folder of your email but without a Nigerian fellow asking to help him with a money transfer.

I have asked to go to this bit because I want to get my daughter some gold studs for earrings. She's 10 now and we said she could have her ears pierced when she was ten. How the hell did she get so old?

This is quite a mission for me as I have a severe phobia of Jewelry. It's not a joke, honest. It petrifies me and I've even had therapy to discover what the root cause was. It's known as Kosmemophobia, Nikola Tesla suffered from it as well. Even as I write this I can feel myself getting nervous. Each window of each shop is draped in gold chains and I start to lose my nerve. Luckily the several gentlemen trying to sell me fake Rolex's draw me away from my fears and I enter into a conversation with one saying how my £14.95 orange Casio is doing just fine.

Amelie goes into one shop for me and soon a deal is done. I have the treasure wrapped and put into a little bag. I have, with the help of my friends, achieved my mission. Now let's get the hell out of here!

We get the water-taxi back and I enter a state of what can only be described as total bliss. I know I'll be seeing my wife and child tomorrow and I miss them but for the moment, the water is calm, the sun shines off the river and its warmth reflects onto my face. Several Mosques are on the horizon and then I hear the call to prayer sounding out across the city. It is an amazing experience. I'm not religious in any way but the chance of the sun, the light shining off the water and the sound of the Imam calling across the city, intensifies my feeling of happiness. Damn it's good to be alive. I vow to do some more traveling soon. This time with my gang though.

At this exact moment Amelie, a keen photographer, sneaks a quick photo. In it I look very happy. For once this isn't a lie.

We briefly visit a local museum which has several artefacts from the history of the area and

Dubai. My favorite being a book written in 1806 by an Everard Home Esq, Its title is supreme.

'Observations on the Camels Stomach respecting the water it contains and the reservoirs in which that fluid is enclosed, with an account of some peculiarities in the Urine.'

We return to Castle Langdon and too soon I am packed and must be off to my final gig. I give the girls a hug and Laurance drives me to the venue.

There, sitting having a cigarette is Iain. Iain was my comrade at arms at University and best man at my wedding. It makes perfect sense that he should just be here on his way through for a Christmas break in Australia. I think I've met more University friends in four days visiting Dubai than I have in 14 years in my own country.

The gig is well attended but it's a quiet smiling crowd. They seem to be enjoying it but they're a lot quieter than the night before. Consequently I go into overdrive and try harder to get a bigger reaction from them. I reach the end and have no idea what their reaction will be. Thankfully it seems to have worked, I count 2 people crying (I can only hope with happiness from the story) and one chap stands up to give me a standing ovation!

He is on his own for it though and soon sits back down quickly. As I walk around to pack up my stuff, quietly smug that all the gigs have thankfully gone well here and older lady catches my eye.

"Thank you for that. It was… different."

A quick message from the comedy gods there to remind me never to be complacent.

I say my goodbyes to Ray and Salman who have done a fantastic job promoting the show and bringing me out here. They run some lovely gigs and if you're a comic on your way through or heading that way I'd give them a shout at dubailaughing.com – Excellent fellows.

I say good bye to Laurance and he heads home and then Iain and I decide to grab some food from somewhere.

I sit in a Chinese restaurant. Opposite me is my friend. Behind him is a Christmas tree and to my left is the skyline of Dubai. Naturally in the background Cliff Richard's 'Mistletoe & Wine' plays. I laugh my head off. We say our goodbyes and I get into a cab to the airport.

Dubai speeds by and it all hits me at once. All my life I wanted to be a stand-up comedian and to make people laugh. This week, it feels like I'm finally on my way. It's a few minutes before I realise I'm crying. I'm going home and I'm so happy.

Thank you Dubai. Good night.

NEXT WEDNESDAY

Bob woke up. This didn't surprise him, as it was
what he usually did most mornings at this time.
In fact very little surprised Bob. It was one of the
few qualities that he had. His unsurpriserbility.
Since childhood his parents had been often vexed
by his ability to remain unaffected by their efforts
on his birthdays. Even the time when they had
moved him during his sleep and had put him in a
tent in the garden.

Not that Bob didn't know how to have fun. Don't
get me wrong. Bob was a very fun bloke who had
a reasonable amount of friends for someone of
his age and was considered to be fun to have
around. It's just that nothing came as a surprise to
him.

He pulled the duvet out of the way and sat up.
Another unsurprising day lay before him.
Bathroom, work, drink in the evening and then
back home for a cup of tea and then bed. It wasn't
much but Bob enjoyed it.

Bob went over to the window and pulled back his
curtains and found much to his surprise, that he
was surprised. He was surprised for two reasons.
One that it wasn't the usual view that always
greeted him and two because he realised that he

had about two seconds left to live.

Now the view that always greeted Bob in the mornings was of his street and the woman in number thirty-seven who always seemed to be getting dressed at that time in the morning. Needless to say this started Bob's day off quite well. Especially as the woman at number thirty seven had seemingly never thought about closing her curtains when getting changed. However this morning, Bob was greeted with the sight of a Roman Legion marching towards him. Well that and a boulder that had been launched by a catapult that was heading directly for him. While not actually known for his mathematical genius Bob quickly calculated that he could either move at the speed of around seventy three miles an hour and get out of the way or he could just stand there and swear. He swore.

"Shit."

This was unusual because Bob never swore. For a brief second Bob wished that his final words had been something a bit more profound but he rationalised very quickly that life, especially his, was too short.

"Fu...."

The phone rang.
It did that.
A lot.

It couldn't be blamed. That was its job. People phoned, it rang but still Gary couldn't bring himself to like it. Gary gave this some thought. He wasn't sure if it was because he hated the phone itself or just the ring. He'd much preferred it when phones had dials and had a bell inside them but since everything had gone electronic you just got this digital blast. This wouldn't be so bad but Gary's phone was worse. His spoke to him.

"Gary, it's for you. Gary, I'm ringing. C'mon Gary pick me up. This hurts."

The problem was that Gary's' phone was possessed. For some reason the spirit of his phones previous owner had decided to stay. Gary had asked him once why.

"Hammond?"

"Detective Hammond."

"Sorry, Detective Hammond?"

"Yes Gary."

"Why have you stayed here in this phone and not, like, you know, gone off to another astral plane or something?"

"Well Gary, It's just there comes a time in your life when you just realise that you never got the opportunity to be really useful, you know. I just felt that maybe if I stuck around for a bit then I could be of more use."

Needless to say Gary had thought about asking the phone, sorry, detective Hammond why he chose to help by possessing a phone but there never seemed to be the right opportunity. He knew that life as a police detective in the relatively inconsequential town of Sunbourne was far from riveting, but if he died Gary was sure that if he must come back as a phone then he'd chose one that a, was in a very busy area and b, was operated by a stunning woman who with any luck had what could only be described as a staggering cleavage.

Putting questions of his phones existential existence aside Gary picked up the receiver and tried to ignore the words of thanks that were emanating from it. It was an internal call from the Desk sergeant, Sarge. He had been at the desk for so long that no one was exactly sure as to what his real name was but he seemed happy to be called by his title. The police station in Sunbourne, like the town itself, was certainly a weird place and you had to forego the eccentricities that it's inhabitants displayed. The Sarge was unfortunately obsessed with using the internal phone system. Not so bad you may think but as the Sarge was only in the next room and that Sunbourne's police station had only three rooms and one of them doubled up as a kitchen/bathroom then his obsession seemed a bit strange. Especially as the door was always open. This led to any phone conversations coming through to Gary in a rough form of stereo. Which was lucky in itself, as the Sarge had the most monotonous voice in the world and anything that might make a conversation with the man less tedious tended to help.

"Yes" said Gary without putting the phone to his ear.

"There's been a suspicious death sir." droned the Sarge.

"Really?" said Gary " A real suspicious death or one like last year?"

"That could have been suspicious sir."

Gary remembered the death last year. An eighty-nine year old gent by the name of Albert Watkins had fallen down dead of seemingly natural causes in the local supermarket. The Sarge had become convinced that the man was killed by foul means. Gary had tried to explain to him that a man dying in the breakfast food aisle, although occurring around cereal did not mean that it was the work of a serial killer and his attempt to rectify the Sarges' baffling understanding of the English language fell on stony ground . The Sarge was not convinced and to this day felt that Gary should have investigated the matter further. Gary chose to ignore this point and let the Sarge give him the details of the suspicious death.

"What's suspicious about it then?"

"He was killed with a boulder, sir."

"A boulder?"

"Yes sir." said the Sarge so matter of factly that Gary was almost convinced that death by boulder was a regular occurrence.

Gary took the details and set off to investigate. Well he set off. Investigation was something that appeared on the television and certainly not in Sunbourne. Things just didn't happen there. Well things of a nature that required a police presence. Gary often wondered what he had done to be placed there.

He put it down to the one day in training when during a riot simulation Gary had tried to diffuse the situation by building a campfire and singing songs. Gary had passed the test purely on his singing ability but it was thought best for his own safety that he was given a nice safe assignment.

So that is how Gary Pearson found himself at the rank of detective at the age of 28. He would have made the news due to the fact that he was the youngest police detective ever but the national press had tried to find Sunbourne and got lost on the way. Instead Gary's story appeared in a tabloid newspaper on page 14 underneath the weather report and next to a letter from a young lady who was concerned about her husbands premature ejaculation. Gary had been quite proud of the newspaper clipping and had stuck it on the wall. Unfortunately the larger headline that read " I WANT A MAN THAT CAN" tended to get the wrong reaction from visitors.

Gary got into his car. A very old Ford Cortina that was considered racy by Sunbourne standards. Mind you a snail that felt the need to carry not only its shell but a small aircraft carrier would be considered racy.

It took Gary twenty minutes to travel what would normally be a five-minute drive anywhere else, because he was stuck behind a caravan. Gary had seen the caravan around before. In fact he had never seen it parked up. It was as though the driver was constantly searching for one of the many caravan parks that populated the region. Gary got out of the car and made his way into Bob's house. The ambulance men were sitting around smoking and looking very pale. In fact they looked as though they would rather be sitting at home and watching daytime TV. Gary took this as a bad sign as most people would rather have root canal work with no anaesthetic than watch daytime TV.

Gary entered the room to see a rather large boulder sitting in the middle of the room. It actually looked quite peaceful, like a rather deformed coffee table. Gary was thinking that it might be difficult to balance a cup of coffee on it but it had a certain something. That something was the four limbs sticking out from underneath it.

Gary looked out at what was left of the window. Well it was more of a round hole now but from the debris that was lying around Gary could see that it did once have double-glazing. Very important that. Kept the draft out.

He looked at the limbs. He knew that the Sarge was right about this one. This was very suspicious and just a little weird.

Gary noticed something. There was no blood.

"Where's the blood?"

"Still in him I think." said Davis, Sunbornes' very own Doctor.

"Oh dear." said another ambulance man as he

dashed towards the door.

Gary went over to the window. Outside he could see his car, the ambulance and three of its attendants all looking as though they would rather be on This Morning.

On the other side he saw Number 37. Gary was no stranger to trigonometry as he had taken the subject at GCSE and had had gained a grade 2. Therefore he was pretty sure that the bolder came from the kitchen of the opposite house.

Coming out of the house Gary crossed the street and walked over to the house. There was no sign of any kind of disturbance and no sign of anyone who lived there.

There was nothing else for it.

He was left with no option.

He'd have to ask the Sarge to check the Free Roaming Data Dispensing Provider, (FRDDP). 20 minutes later after fumbling with a pay phone while the Sarge checked in the FRDDP or phone book, as it was more commonly known, Gary discovered that the occupant of No. 37 was a Miss Lucy Winters.

The planets rested in the ever-expanding swirl that was the Cosmos. In an area of one galaxy commonly known as the "Arse end of the Universe", (That is the part not called Uxbridge) an energy mass started to collect and form. The energy mass had been dormant for some time, though unaware of this the mass started to take its natural shape. That of a woman.

The creator of all life stifled a yawn and vowed never to use the snooze button again. The effect of these infernal machines had caused many to oversleep. The creator of all life had overslept by about 50,000 years. This was the problem with being an immortal. The time just flew by. It wasn't as if she had just sat around for a bit. She'd actually achieved quite a lot. So there had been a few mistakes. Jupiter was supposed to have been a foot spa and she was beginning to become aware of a phenomenon known as a 'Fast Food Chicken Outlet.'

This was another problem with being the Creator of all Life. Not only was she immortal she was also omnipresent and omnipotent. If she wanted to go somewhere she was already there and she knew everything that had happened. It really put the notion of holidays into perspective. No finding a charming little bistro while on holiday for her because she had not only created it but had also designed the menu.

Needless to say being a woman once a month she would suffer the same fate as all women. This was a bit of a mistake on her part. It was during the development process that she started the symptoms that would plague all women. She felt sorry for this technical glitch that she had inflicted on females. Many a cry she had heard from the female of species throughout the universe. She tried to amend the situation but was only reminded of it once a month and at the time she would find herself just all over the place. One of the side effects of being omnipresent and pre-menstrual. Bummer.

She could of course go back in time and change things as she saw fit. It wasn't really time travel as we imagine it. It was more like going back to check you'd turned the cooker off when you went out even though you haven't left yet. It wasn't as if she would meet herself there either as she found that she was omnipresent at all times. Even Bank holidays.

She needed a break. She decided that a visit to her favourite place was in order. An insignificant planet that contained many life-forms that were under the illusion that they were far more important than they actually were. As a result of their audacious attitude the Creator of all life decided to teach them a lesson. She decided to leave them alone and not interfere with their way of life. Unfortunately she instigated this plan before she realised that these beings did not have the same lifespan as her, so they never really got the point. Hope though, always sprung eternal. Maybe one day they would understand. Actually she knew that the day in question would be June the 23rd in the year 2634. Another problem she suffered was that it was pretty tricky to surprise herself. Then again it wasn't as if there was any other omnipresent beings around who could surprise her.

She drifted round the planet and entered the thoughts and minds of its inhabitants. It was

when she passed over the Northern Hemisphere
she began to notice something strange. In a small
sea-side town events seemed to be taking place of
a startling nature. They were startling because for
the first time she didn't know what would
happen.

The grass curled up around her pink tracksuit as
she lay on the ground. She was at peace. She was
perfectly relaxed. She was at one with the world.
She was Eighty-Four.

She was Mrs Uckbourne.

Around her she could hear the sound of children
playing and laughing. She looked down past her
feet and saw the kids. There was about five of
them. One of them seemed to glow in a weird
way. Not evil, but certainly out of place.
Further away she could make out a man walking
towards them. The children parted and the man
approached Mrs Uckbourne. She could make out
he was wearing a RAF uniform. She stood up
and straightened out the pink tracksuit. She then
turned around and held her arms out to the man.
They embraced. It was Mr Uckbourne. He'd been
dead since 1935.
"Hello Mrs Uckbourne."
"Hello Mr Uckbourne."
As they held each other she felt the years slip
away. This was the moment she lived for. In
every dream Albert would return and ask her to

come with him. She didn't know where and she didn't know why. All she knew was that she wasn't ready yet. She declined once again his offer. They sat down next to each other and watched the children they never had, play.

The child that glowed slightly took it upon herself to disappear at this point. Reforming herself into her chosen form, The Creator of all life decided to leave Mrs Uckbourne to enjoy her peace and take a look around the town. Besides she knew that the doorbell was about to ring and disturb the old lady's sleep.

As Gary was still pondering the trajectory of the boulder and beginning to think that an evening class in advanced algebra might help, Lucy Winters was parking her car on the far side of town. She pulled up the hand brake and let out a long sigh. It was a sigh that could be interpreted in many ways. Most of those interpretations would be negative and they would be right. Lucy was worried about Mr. Collins and his leg. Sunbourne was very popular with old people. They retired here to be by the sea and get away from the hustle and bustle of their working lives. They came by their hundreds. This meant that Sunbourne's only growth industry was care work. It all started in 1872 when the ageing Lord Anthony Propwell, 32nd cousin to Queen

Victoria, visited the town and declared that the fresh air and invigorating sea water had made him feel like a new man. This declaration was seized upon by the towns' folk and soon Sunbourne became a tourist haven. The fact that Lord Propwell was clinically insane and regularly declared that he was a new woman called Edith was glossed over as it was felt that advertising the fact that the bracing air and invigorating sea water was beneficial to men with gender identity crisis' would not help the tourist trade.

So Lucy Winters was kept very busy visiting the towns old folk and helping them with their lives. A smile formed on her face when she realised that Mr Collins and his leg was one of the downsides of her job. She was about to visit one of her more positive patients. In fact Mrs Uckbourne was probably the most positive.

After rising from her sleep Mrs Uckbourne answered the door and ushered Lucy in. Within minutes a large mug of tea and several sandwiches were placed in front of her, as was their now weekly routine. After the first few months of visiting the sprightly octogenarian Lucy soon realised that she undoubtedly got more from the experience than her gracious host, as Mrs Uckbourne filled the young care worker in on all the gossip that was going on.

Mrs Uckbourne had led a varied and exciting life but like most old people she didn't feel the need to brag endlessly about it. Instead she tended to marvel at the wonder of her new replacement hip and the freedom that it had brought back into her life. For the first few visits, Lucy had carried Mrs Uckbourne's case file with her but the vast collection of notes weighed as much as five bags of sugar and had started to give Lucy a bad back. So instead she took it home and occasionally read its detailed notes whenever she was feeling uninspired. Mrs Uckbourne's life had the effect of cheering up anyone who had heard it.

Mrs Uckbourne's husband, James, was a test pilot for the RAF who sadly died in a crash during the first year of their marriage in 1935. The distraught widowers grief was further compounded by the fact that the plane that he had been flying was so secret that his death was covered up and she was never allowed to even have a funeral for him. The cover up had been so extensive that when in September 1939 War was declared Call up papers arrived at Mrs Uckbourne's doorstep. She looked at the papers for a long time and did what any right-minded patriot would do. She cut her hair, taped down her breasts and joined the RAF where she soon became embroiled in the Battle for Britain. Having shot down four German fighters and finding that several of her colleagues were rather worried about their feelings for their fellow comrade in arms, she was shot down over France. Finding her way through occupied territory she managed to hook up with the Resistance where her true identity was discovered and she was soon placed in Paris, where she gained the eye of an influential German Colonel and found herself working in the German high command. After several years of passing information back to Whitehall and rising up the ladder of her German employers, Mrs Uckbourne was transferred to Berlin where it was said that she worked in the upper echelons of the third Reich. Her time after the end of the war was shrouded in secrecy although it was believed that the Russians captured her where upon she found herself in the Kremlin. These were of course rumours that were never proved. Lucy had asked her boss once how Sunbourne social services had such detailed files on their residents. He had responded with a subtle wink and the statement "We have detailed files."

Lucy was distracted by Mrs Uckbourne returning from the kitchen with yet more sandwiches.

"I'm sorry?" said Lucy.

"My party. You are coming aren't you?"

There were many things in this world that Lucy could predict but one of them she couldn't would be a party at Mrs Uckbourne's. That should be something to look forward to and to dispel any thoughts of Mr Collins and his leg.

The creator of all life walked down the street and crossed over to join the crowd, narrowly avoiding being run over by a caravan that trundled past out of nowhere. There was a group of about fifty or so people milling around trying to look concerned and not quite so fascinated by the crane that had now arrived outside the house of Bob.

As she looked at the scene she realised that she was experiencing confusion for the first time. It was a weird feeling that gnawed at her insides at a constant rate. She knew little things. She knew that a boulder had killed a young man. She knew that the boulder had come from somewhere other than this time-line but as to why or how remained a mystery.

Looking back to the building she saw a young man exit from the house walking backwards and unraveling a large tape measure at the same time. She knew at that point that the young man was trying to work out the trajectory of the boulder. She was about to offer to help, as mathematics was one of her top hobbies when the young man stopped. Turned his head over to the crowd and looked directly at her. He smiled and then returned to his backwards perambulation.

The creator of all life remained routed to the spot. Terrified, worried, confused and with a strange new feeling in her stomach. It was then that she realised that she had been blushing.

After jotting down several notes in his book and trying in vain to work out if he'd made a mistake, Gary realised that the boulder had come from within the kitchen or the upstairs bathroom of number 37. Well either of those two or it had come from the direct result of a Butterfly flapping its wings in China and a freak Tsunami in the region of Skegness. Gary vowed never to use Chaos theory in his mathematics again.

As he stood there trying to make sense of the days events two things stuck in his mind. How could a boulder travel from someone's kitchen, leave no damage, killing a young man on the other side of a street and who was that woman he smiled at? There was clearly a lot of thinking that needed to be done and in Sunbourne when you needed to think there was only one place you went to. Gary knew that a visit to see Dennis was on the cards.

Rome wasn't built in a day. In fact it took many generations of labour to create the empire that spanned nearly the entire known world at the time. It was a fact that was greatly acknowledged by many great warriors and theologians, then and now. As the soldiers of the Roman Empire strode across Europe they knew in their hearts that the goal they sought may not happen within their lifetime or even the next. But still they marched on. To the north they traveled and to the east, west and south and met resistance wherever they went. It just took time that's all. It was this knowledge that General Lucidicus Julius told himself that very morning when the battle began.

Though he was not happy.

He was not happy for several reasons.

Firstly he had been promised the Germania
campaign and he knew that the battle with the
Goths of the North would bring himself, his
family and the Empire great honour. He knew
that the campaign would be his great mark on the
world. He would be talked about for future
generations as grandfathers sat with their
grandchildren and told of the just but fair Roman
general who led the soldiers bravely into war.
Secondly he missed his wife and kids. He had
been traveling for over three months now and
knew that the battle ahead could last for over a
year. Then once the campaign had succeeded he
would have to take control of the conquered land
and govern it until Rome sent his replacement.
Thirdly he was not happy because this land that
he stood upon did not feel right. There was no
tension as he and his troops landed. Usually there
was a mass of locals stood upon the shoreline
ready to fight to the death to protect the land that
they loved. But this time there was no one except
an old man who was walking a dog.
General Lucidicus Julius marched bravely to the
frail old man and stood before him trying to
ignore the dog that was sniffing where he
shouldn't be.
"I am General Lucidicus Julius of the Roman
Army, Chief standard bearer of the might of the
Empire. And I have come to conquer this land
and slay all who would stand in the way of the

progress that is known as Rome!" said the General in his most conquering voice.

"That's nice." Said the old man. Who seemed to be more concerned as to the activities of his dog and why the big soldier hadn't attempted to shoo the animal away in that embarrassing way you have to when a pet is sniffing your crotch.

"Will you be staying long?"

Lucidicus had begun to wonder of it was such a good idea to let his second in command pick the landing spot, but he realised that it was his own fault for being sentimental when his Commander had said that it looked like a good spot for swimming.

The forth reason for his unhappy state truly baffled him. He had travelled far and had seen most things that would make any normal man quake in fear. He had witnessed the assault on the low lands of France. He had been in the thick of battle in Spain and had eaten at the restaurant owned by Romulus Donaculus (It doesn't matter what century you're in, fast food is always a risky business) but he had never seen anything like the events that had happened since the battle finally started this morning. To begin with the first boulder of the day had shot through the air in what seemed to be a perfect trajectory and had disappeared into thin air and then there was a flash of light. The light was so bright that the great soldier had to shield his eyes from its intensity. When he opened them he was a little perturbed to discover that he was no longer on the battlefield but in a strange place. A place which was very quiet and had peculiar buildings, but this was not disturbed him the most. It was when he saw a horseless carriage pulling a large white box behind it that his fear took hold of him. He ran and while he ran tried to wonder how quickly he could get back to Rome.

10 Films

with

my

Dad

Acknowledgements

Following are a list of names that if you are on may prove interesting. If by some miracle I don't know you and your still reading this then I can only apologise for putting you through the following. (Which I mean the list of acknowledgements not the actual book, which would make this, the worst advert ever)

I'd like to thank Mum & Dad obviously for providing me with so much material. Emma & Billie for being an inspiration. Jill Edwards for her guidance. Rob Dumbrell, Romesh Ranganathan, Rue Barratt & Sam Savage for being in the show via films.

Also thanks to all those who joined in but ended up on the cutting room floor Sean McLoughlin, Jim Holland, Bill Gleave, Kerry Herbert & Roz Ryan. Katie Wells took the photo's on the front of Kimble & I.

The exceptional cover design is by David Jordan

My lovely daughter Rosie for coming on the Edinburgh adventure and also of course, Kimble the dog who stole the show and still does every day.

Thanks also to all the audiences that came to see the show and laughed.

Finally I'd like to thank and dedicate this book to my wife Jennie who has been my best friend, supporter and inspiration. Thank you for all the laughs and also one day in September 2010 saying 'Maybe you should use the dog?'

Chapter 1

The Greatest Story Ever Told

This is a story about communication. It's about how my father & I never talked.

We only ever watched films.

It's ok though there is a happy ending so stick with it. This isn't going to be several hours' worth of reading followed by a massive downer of regret and lost opportunities.

I hate that.

Nothing gets me more riled than a good story spoiled at the end by a depressing ending. Like 'The Departed.' (Martin Scorsese 2008) 2 hours I sat through the film and in the end everyone dies. Everyone except Mark Wahlberg and an obvious visual rat metaphor.

How can this be? Don't get me wrong I don't mind bad guys winning or good guys being a little rough around the edges, it's just that I love films. It was how I was brought up. Consequently I just get angry if the love I've given these characters is just thrown away at the end.

Also it doesn't go on too long. It hasn't been strung out so that it can be extended into a trilogy. If like me you thought that 'Lord of The Rings' was a nine hour film about walking and sat there thinking 'Why didn't they just take the giant eagles to Mount Doom. There are giant eagles. Where did they keep the giant eagles. FRICKIN GIANT EAGLES!" then this should be for you.

Also no one dies at the end and most importantly at all none of it is in 3D.

I guess I'm trying to say that I hope you'll enjoy the story because nearly all of it is true and it's like a movie but in paper form.

I guess the root of our communication problems was a generational one. Dad was born in 1941 during World War 2 when men were 'MEN.' I was born in 1971. Where men had long hair, wore flairs and were obsessed by fondue. It was also a time where men thought that Freddy Mercury was just a little bit flamboyant.

But not Dad. Dad had been a chief engineer in the navy and had undoubtedly encountered many flamboyant men in his time.

It may seem silly now but life was not as free (not that it still couldn't use a bit more freedom) as it is now. We had no idea. Yeah he was a little bit camp but come on, he was a rock god. When he finally came out, sadly days before his death, most people were shocked. The same can be said of Elton John. ('But he married Rene!' said a distraught Elton fancying female friend)

This is what we project and want in our stars. We want the chance, however slight, that we may be able to be with or know them in some way more than on our screen. This is the immediacy of modern media. We see them right there on the screen so often we feel as if we know them and consequently project our own beliefs on them. Also when we read that Gwyneth Paltrow has split with Brad Pitt it won't be long before she's ringing your doorbell. (Curse that Chris Martin for getting in the way)

And in the 70's attitudes to different lifestyles were sadly not as advanced as they are now. Consequently Dads biggest fear when I was born was that I would grow up to be gay.

I should in all honesty tell you that I now live in Brighton. Considered by many to be the gay capital of the world. Think San Francisco but without the Bridge.

I am not however gay. I just like to annoy dad.

Even today though and even in Brighton homophobia sadly still exists.

I have a little dog called Masie and an 8 year old daughter too so everything has to be pink. One morning I was out walking my little dog with her pink lead when I bumped into a man. I apologised. He looked at me. Looked at the dog. Noted her lead & collar, then looked back at me.

'Gay!" he sneered.

Now you know in life when you think of a suitable response but it's usually 24 hours later? This was the first time I'd ever thought of one straightaway.

I looked at him in shock.

Looked at the dog.

Looked back at him and said,

"I don't know. I've never asked her before?"

And then I punched the bigot in the face and ran way. (I didn't of course. Like all bigots he was not endowed with the greatest IQ so I used the time it was taking to work out what I said to make my escape.)

Back in 1971 Dad had a plan. A plan to ensure my masculinity.

It was a 2-fold plan. First he would make sure I watched every single John Wayne film ever made & secondly he would buy me weapons. Lots of weapons. There was a boy called Chris Hardy, he lived ten doors up from us and was only 2 months older than me and for his 5th birthday he got a Grifter bicycle. It was awesome. It was the pinnacle of technology and above all else it was cool. It was the coolest thing ever made. It was brown (this was the 70's, everything was brown even pants.) and had gold flames on the bodywork and I wanted one.

I wanted one like I had never wanted anything before in my life.

So I started my campaign. Being 5 years old my campaign quickly reduced itself to begging constantly day & night for it.

"Can I get a Grifter?"

"Eat your breakfast"

"Can I get a Grifter?"

"Put your seatbelt on."

"Can I get a Grifter?"

"Eat your dinner."

"Can I get a Grifter?"

"FOR THE LOVE OF ALL THINGS HOLY CAN YOU AT LEAST STOP TO BREATHE?"

Surely 2 months of constant begging would result in my goal. What I didn't know was that Dad had already analysed the situation. You see as an engineer his brain works in very specific controlled manner. He will look at any situation and apply strict controlled questions and several laws of physics to get his answer. Also the fact that he knows absolutely everything there is to know about everything helps.

This had helped him to rise to the level of Chief Engineer, that and shouting a lot. I don't mean in an aggressive way at all, it's just that my father is exceptionally English and is therefore exceptionally loud in a way that only exceptionally English men can be.

I remember when we went to America and we were sat right at the back of the plane. My father gave me a quick lesson on flight engineering by whispering in my ear,

"THOSE WINGS WILL MOVE AT LEAST EIGHT FEET UP & DOWN DURING FLIGHT BUT WILL BE UNDER THE MOST STRESS DURING TAKE OFF. SO YOU SEE THE ADVANTAGE OF US BEING AT THE BACK MEANS THAT IF WE BREAK UP ON TAKE OFF. FROM HERE, WE'LL HAVE THE BEST VIEW!"

Never boring travelling with my Dad and you usually get to meet the Air Marshall.

When I woke up on that morning I didn't know that my father had already checked out the Grifter bicycle and had found it to be unsuitable for purpose (a fact born out as the Grifter was notoriously heavy, lacked any suspension and would be soon overtaken by the far popular BMX style of bikes) so he had made other purchases. On July 13th 1976 while Chris Hardy was undoubtedly hugging his Grifter I went down stairs to discover that Dad had bought me an air rifle and a hunting knife.

Seriously he bought his 5 year old what would now be described as offensive weapons. This was the 70's in a time before health & safety executives had taken over. I was lucky Dad hadn't bought me a nuclear bomb,

"YOU SEE SON THIS IS THE ADVANTAGE OF HAVING A ONE MEGATON DEVICE. IT'S EASY TO TRANSPORT AND COMES EQUIPED WITH A FULL PRIMING KIT. NO OFF YOU GO AND PLAY."

Dad was very excited and quickly set up a target on one of the trees in the back garden and filmed me on his Super8 camera as I manfully popped away at the target.

15 years later the tree died of lead poisoning. Mother was furious and accused me. I in turn blamed dad so he dug out the old Super8 film and like some bizarre homage to Kevin Costner in JFK acted as prosecutor in my trial.

"AND HERE WE CAN CLEARLY SEE AIDAN SHOOTING THE TREE. AND THE TREE MOVES BACK AND TO THE LEFT. BACK AND TO THE LEFT. BACK AND TO THE LEFT."

When I wasn't destroying the environment we would watch films. This was a glorious time for watching films on TV in the years before soap operas took over the schedules and it took ages for films to emerge onto our screens. There were only three channels (BBC1, BBC2 and ITV) and they only started at 12pm and showed old films by the bucket load.

Dad would sit us down or me and my sister would sit ourselves down if dad was away working and watch every classic film we could. From black & white movies starring Cary Grant or James Stuart to musicals to westerns to war films to Sci-Fi to Basil Rathbone Sherlock Holmes films. We would soak up every film we possibly could.

I remember fondly a few years later my sister babysitting and us both staying up to watch The Godfather whilst eating chips from the takeaway and being scared by the dead horses head.

So naturally there was always a John Wayne film on. My dad was a huge fan and consequently I had to be one to. This was a true Hollywood star and also before the time when Public Enemy told me he was racist.

We would have Sunday roast and all crash out on the sofa watching a on of his films on TV and the whole family would snooze to the gentle sounds of Wayne annihilating the American Indian population.

So when I got the part of the Centurion in my school nativity play, Father was ecstatic because John Wayne had played the centurion in the 1969 John Huston film 'THE GREATEST STORY EVER TOLD.'

If you've been lucky enough not to see it don't worry. You've missed only 4 hours of turgid Hollywoodised biblical epic. It's an appalling film that has some amazing casting. Max Von Sydow is Jesus and Shelly Winters (she of Poseidon Adventure and Alfie fame) plays Mary Magdalene. John Wayne doesn't appear till the very end when Jesus is on the cross. He walks in, sees Jesus on the cross and says,

'Aw surely he is the son of God."

Although with so many pauses it sounds like,

"Aw... Surely... He... Is... The... Son... of... God."

Legend has it that despite the one line of dialogue Wayne couldn't get it right. John Huston turned to him and said,

"That's brilliant John, brilliant. But it needs more reverence. It needs more awe!"

TAKE 2

"AWWWWWWWWWWWWWWWWWW WWWE Truly… He… is… the … son… of… God!"

So I didn't have a lot of competition in the acting stakes.

Like John Wayne I too had only one line of dialogue, which was,

"Search the village, collect the children!"

This however was not good enough for Dad and so he changed it and coached me to do it in the voice of John Wayne. He changed it to this,

"Well get in that village… and get me those kids!"

He even tried to get me to walk like John Wayne. For those of you who haven't seen a John Wayne film you should know that his primary acting muscles were his shoulders. Think Schwarzenegger but without the gravitas. He would put those shoulders forward and almost fall over with only some sort of gravity defying will preventing him from toppling over. I was 5 years old I couldn't walk like John Wayne, I walked like Norman Wisdom. A drunk Norman Wisdom.

They gave me a centurion helmet that was so large, combined with my crap walk, wobbled on my head so much that when I stopped to deliver my line it fell to the floor. I promptly burst into tears and had to be carried out of the church hall by Dad as I screamed,

"BUT HE IS THE SON OF GOD DAD! HE IS! HE IS!"

On the plus side I was never forced to watch another John Wayne film again.

Chapter 2

Terror in the Aisles

In celebration of my acting debut (I say celebration, I think Mum had taken off for the afternoon and Dad didn't know what else to do.) Dad decided to take me to see my first film at the cinema.

I vividly remember driving past cinemas when I was younger, attracted by the posters and the titles. They looked like massive palaces to me and I was so excited to finally be going to one and with my Dad. I can remember it so clearly even now. We went to our nearest one, the Streatham Odeon. I remember I was wearing shorts and got very excited when Dad bought some popcorn from an old lady behind the counter. She had a white shirt on that was partially covered by a vividly striped waistcoat. Her glasses were on a chain and hung just below her neckline.

Do you remember your first film at the cinema? Chances are it was probably a Disney film. Brilliant works designed to be perfectly safe entertainment for families with children.

It wasn't a Disney film.

Now my Dad as I've said was a naval man and consequently obsessed with all things to do with the sea. I was 5 so the choice to him was obvious.

He took me to see Jaws.

I'm sure you've seen Jaws. Pretty much everyone has. It is an amazingly good film with many great scenes. My particular favourite scene is the one where the 5 year old child... is eaten by the shark.

I didn't sleep for a year.

Dad with his engineering brain however couldn't understand why I was having trouble separating reality from the film to him it made no sense. Now Dad being an educated man he never missed the opportunity to pass on that knowledge at any available moment. So in order to help me get to sleep he gave me a lecture. A lecture that would prove how safe I was from Shark Attack. A lecture on the most common causes of death in 1976.

Number 1 Road traffic accident.

Number 2 Falls.

Number 3 Poisons.

He then ends this lecture with the now legendary sentence,

"SO YOU SEE. YOU'RE MORE LIKELY TO BE RUN OVER BY A BUS ON YOUR WAY TO SCHOOL TOMORROW MORNING... SLEEP WELL.

Needless to say this didn't help.

Now at this point in the show I wanted to show clips from the films in question. Unfortunately it costs a ridiculous amount of money in licensing to show clips so I had a solution. Being as how I'm a massive fan of film. I have a video camera, some friends and more importantly a dog, what could go wrong? Sadly not all my friends were on the same page as me.

Jaws Sketch

INT.   REHERSAL STUDIO
          DAY

4 rather lovely & brilliant comics stand around eating snacks and looking really annoyed.

                    ROB DUMBRELL

          He thinks he's Steven Spielberg

                    RUE BARRATT

          Yeah

                    SAM SAVAGE

He does, it's like he's living in a
bubble. What's he doing?

                    RUE BARRATT

His mental state is denigrating.

                    SAM SAVAGE

I don't like it when he cries when
you tell him something he
doesn't like. That's what gets me,
that's why I don't want to do it.
It's like kicking your nan.

                    ROMESH
                    RANGANATHAN

He's so needy.

                    RUE BARRATT

Like a child.

Off screen we hear

                    AIDAN

                    DUDES!

The camera spins round and we see Aidan
standing at a table. He is holding up his jacket

and behind it something moves. He starts to do the Jaws theme.

AIDAN

Da Dum. Da Dum. Dad dum dadum dadum dada!

He whips back the jacket to reveal…

His dog Kimble, a border terrier. Kimble has a cardboard shark fin attached to his back.

AIDAN(very enthusiastically)

It's the shark!

Cut back to the 4. They look massively unimpressed.

EXT.   BRIGHTON BEACH   DAY

Kimble sits next to Aidan as a ball is waved around.

AIDAN

See! He looks just like a shark!

Aidan throws the ball and Kimble chases after it. His shark fin wobbling as he runs towards the waves.

CUT TO: The 4 who are now standing on the beach.

RUE BARRATT

Shall we just go?

SAM SAVAGE

He's not going to notice.

They walk away.

CUT TO: Kimble, ball in mouth being trounced by a large wave.

END OF SKETCH

Now when I show this sketch people laugh. They laughed and then they feel sorry for my dog. This is a dog whose entire happiness is dependent on jumping in the sea on a daily basis regardless of weather. He is insane.

However stick a fin on it and film him and people look at you like you are evil so here is a picture of him all safe and warm post-shoot in his trailer.

At this point in 1976 I should introduce my mother. She had of course been an integral part of the story so far (what with giving birth etc) but it was at this point that mother stepped in to divert a potential catastrophe. As a witness to Dad's lecture and seeing the look of complete fear on my face, Mum did something that all mums do at some point in their Childs life. She told a little white lie.

Now there's nothing wrong with this and if you think about it this happens all the time. Parents will tell little white lies to make you feel better about things. Like for example. The tooth fairy.

We all in our heart of hearts know that they don't exist but it's a lot nicer thinking that a mythical beastie will come down and reward you for your tooth rather than standing there worried because part of you has fallen out of your head.

So my mum, thinking as quickly as she could, said the first thing she could think of. She after all was there when Dad was off around the world working. She was the one who'd have to deal with the late nights, the nightmares and the lack of sleep.

"Don't worry." She said "You'll always be perfectly safe as long as you always have your red wellies with you."

They were there at the door of my room. My red wellies. Now in fairness to Mum I think she meant that I should be safe with them being in close proximity. I instead chose to wear them. I wore them all the time. I wore them to school. I wore them to bed. I even wore them in the bath.

Well you would there's water in there and one thing we do know is that THERE ARE SHARKS IN THE WATER!

I even wore them when we went on holiday to Greece.

There I was in the full heat of the Mediterranean sun wearing my red wellies and perfectly safe from shark attack. I also found the following picture as well which confused me at first.

It is of me with my sister, yet you can see I am clearly upset by this and I think I know why.

There I am clearly distressed by something whilst standing next to me is my sister who I love very much but if you look closely you can see that while I am wearing my red wellies she is not. AND IS THEREFORE DOOMED!

I would like to point out that I have now reached adulthood and still to this day have a pair of red wellies with me at all times.

And I would like to point out that I have still yet to be attacked by a shark. So if you take nothing else away from this book then it should be to always listen to your mother. She knows stuff.

CHAPTER 3

Darth Vader is a Wuss

This wasn't a bit in the show but I just wanted to say something and chronologically it fits in here. During the show I wanted to say a bit about Star Wars and not in a positive way. It was pointed out to me (quite rightly) that any stuff on Star Wars has been done to death and would detract from the show as it's not one of the films I saw with Dad.

It's just that Darth Vader is a rubbish Villain. There I've said it. He's a cipher to represent the bad guy and cut out from the most basic character arc that fits the Star Wars story. Also any credibility he had as a villain is totally destroyed by the abomination that was the Prequels. A series of films that reduced a really bad guy into a petulant teenage boy with mother issues.

I know Star Wars has its many fans and I don't blame them but my feelings were not helped by having recently seen the scariest villain in movie history on TV mere days before seeing the space epic.

The sad thing is that this character rarely makes various top 10 lists but should be because he makes Darth look like a small boy who shouts 'Yippee' unconvincingly. (oh hang on George Lucas did that already)

It's the character of Bill Sykes played by Oliver Reed in the musical 'OLIVER.'

Yes you read that right. There in the middle of a big Hollywood style musical is the most convincing portrayal of villainy ever. It's as though the director had given Oliver a different script to the one everyone else has got. He is a brutal, murdering thug who scared the living daylights out of me when I saw him. His English bull terrier 'Bullseye' only served to show the merest form of humanity in the character and he just used his charisma to eat up the screen. He also has one of the most exciting and bleak deaths in cinema ever. Check it out.

Chapter 4

History Lessons

When it came to putting together this show I talked to my Dad and asked why we always went to the cinema. It was all we ever seemed to do. Any time we had a spare hour or two and were alone we went. We saw some brilliant films, one Saturday we went to the West End of London to watch 'FLASH GORDON' a film so camp it needed a soundtrack by Queen just to butch it up a bit, and we saw some dross too.

'POPEYE' with Robin Williams was 2 hours that I'm still trying to get back and also 'KRULL' a British fantasy film that had every BRITISH actor ever in it. It holds a special place in my heart as being the first film I'd watched at the cinema and thinking 'Oh this is a bit rubbish isn't it."

Of course I told Dad it was great. He said so too so I must've got it wrong. We talked enthusiastically about it on the way home and when we got back Mum asked Dad what he thought of it. Dad must've thought he was out of earshot because I remember he distinctly telling Mum it was 'Awful.'

I was too young too realise at the time the significance of this. We were at a stage in our relationship where to save any embarrassment we were prepared to lie to make each other happy.

A barrier that had removed itself by the time we saw 'RETURN OF THE JEDI.' I remember the horror in dad's voice when the Ewoks first appeared.

"OH GOD"

I felt his pain and even the Luke / Darth face off couldn't save us from the dire quality control. It was when the once mighty Chewbacca swung onto a Walker while singing out the Tarzan jungle call, I called it quits. The shark had jumped and so had our collective patience.

It was also the first time I had sworn I front of Dad.

"Dad, is it just me or is this utter shit?"

I remember Dad roared with laughter and then told me off for swearing.

It turns out that the reason for all this film watching was a result of Dads own upbringing. Apparently all he ever did with his dad was go to the cinema to avoid conversation. Virtually twice a week Dad would be carted off to the cinema to watch films again and again. The earliest film Dad says he remembers seeing was the now classic World War 2 propaganda film 'WENT THE DAY WELL?'

Consequently I've had to watch it with Dad about a million times and I still love it.

If you haven't seen it yet then you are missing out on an absolute classic. It stars Thora Hird amongst others,

SHOOTING NAZIS!

Honesty if you thought 'Songs of Praise' was her highpoint you haven't seen anything till you've seen Thora with a Webley shooting indiscriminately at the attacking enemy.

The plot concerns a group of German paratroopers who, disguised as English troops, have to capture and hold hostage and entire British village. A village by the way that is populated by the most frightfully plucky people you've ever met.

Now chances are you seen plenty of films in which either the good guys or bad guys are in disguise and are rumbled by a simple thing they never accounted for. When doing the show at this point I always ask the audience if they can guess how the Germans are rumbled?

There have been many suggestions from accents to eating Bratwurst in public but none have ever got it right. Have a think, see if you can guess because I'm wiling to bet unless you've seen the film you never will.

They are actually foiled by a bar of chocolate.

I'm not making this up. The scene is an acting master class of understatement.

POSH WOMAN: "My that's odd. This bar of chocolate just fell out of Corporal Hendersons rucksack!"

POSH MAN: "Well what's so odd about that?"

POSH WOMAN: "Well it says..."

THERE IS NOW A PAUSE SO LONG YOU COULD FIT THE ENTIRE D DAY LANDINGS THROUGH IT.

POSH WOMAN CONT. "It says Chocolade!"

POSH MAN: "But that's how they spell Chocolate in Germany. Why would Corporal Henderson have German chocolate...UNLESS!"

And from that they kill them all.

It's really put me off shopping at LIDL.

It does of course beg the question, since when has chocolate been a tool in major detective work?

INT.   DINING ROOM
          EVENING

Black & white film.

We see the 4 suspects all sitting around the table at a dinner party. The Detective stands at one end opposite our view with two either side. From the angle of the camera we can not see who is sitting just below us.

DETECTIVE

The reason why I've called you all here tonight is that I believe one of you...

In turn we cut to each dinner guest as they give best shock reactions to what the detective is saying.

DETECTIVE

... is a German spy!

All four instantly look shocked and turn to face each other and then look to camera.

CUT TO: The fifth guest is Kimble the dog who is eating from the plate in front of him. It is covered in sweets and chocolates.

(Those of you that are keen dog enthusiasts and are already calling the RSPCA fear not. The advantage of filming in black & white is that mini sausages look a little like chocolates)

Now you'd think following that lesson and my own childhood I would have learned something wouldn't you?

I have a daughter now called Rosie and if you have a child yourself you'll know a certain fact. By the time your child reaches the age of about 6, you begin to realise something. Something you never thought could happen. It's the cold hard fact that when if you have to watch another animation you're going to go absolutely bus stop mental.

The tempting lure of slightly more grown up films is just on the horizon and one day one of those films came on TV and I remember seeing it when I was roughly the same age as my daughter.

Dad of course took me to see the film. It was great. We loved it. We loved it so much that straight after Dad took me to a shop so I could get a jacket so I could look like the hero. Then shortly after Dad bought himself a hat so he could look like the hero.

Now the film never did me any harm so surely it would be perfectly acceptable to show my daughter 'RAIDERS OF THE LOST ARK?'

Have you any idea how many people get shot in the head in that film? Obviously more than zero is too much for a 6 year old. I'd even made that classic mistake parents make when showing films and completely forgot about the melty face bit at the end but it was ok in the end. We didn't have any nightmares because Rosie just laughed. Phew. All was OK.

Until the next day when I got a phone call from school telling me that during the lunch hour Rosie had removed her belt and was whipping Nazis heads off in the playground.

I had inadvertently created a 6-year-old Nazi hunter. Which in the long run I didn't think was such a bad thing. But I walked away suitably chastised and thought nothing more of it. Until 3 weeks later the school was doing a production of 'THE SOUND OF MUSIC.'

I have never been so scared in my life.

I sat there in sheer horror as my child, who was playing one of the infinite number of children of the Von Trapp family, (Primary school productions usually have multiple actors playing each part. It does give everyone a turn and keeps eager parents happy. It does however do nothing for making ay sense of the narrative) arrived on stage. What would she do when the Nazis turned up? I needn't have worried because the school dealt with it brilliantly by cutting the Nazis out completely!

It became a rather turgid boring love story. At the end Rosie came up to me.

"Did you enjoy that daddy?"

"Yes, of course but it was a bit different from the film, as in the film, there are Nazis."

Rosie paused as she thought this last statement through and then her face lit up as she realised what this statement meant.

"Indiana Jones is in the sound of music!"

If you think about it that would quite possibly be the best film ever.

Chapter 5

Quality Time

I guess another reason why we may have had difficulty communicating was that Dad & I didn't really have a lot of quality time together. This was mostly due to Dad travelling around the globe on various engineering projects. There were however one thing that if Dad was in town we would always do and that was always on Thursday nights BBC2 at 6pm. The 6pm slot on a weekday was the best moment for kids. Dinner and homework (yeah, right!) had been done and they had the best things on. Usually old Black & white short films like Flash Gordon with Buster Crabbe or my personal favourite Basil Rathbone as Sherlock Holmes.

This was I think a golden time for television. There were only three channels, BBC's 1 & 2 and ITV and that was it. Satellite TV & the internet had yet to beam in from the skies and Channel 4 was a long distant dream of teenage boys to come.

Rumour has it Channel 4 would be showing naughty foreign films late at night causing adolescent guys to stay up late into the night praying that erotica would soon be displayed. It's important to note that teenage boys at the time equated a brief flash of breasts in a French new wave film to be a naughty foreign film. I personally remember tuning in my black & white portable TV to Channel 4 one night with my headphones on, so as not to be found out by the parents. The film that I had cunningly deduced as being a total nudey fest was 'LAST YEAR AT MARIENBAD' which started at 11:45! Surely this would be a winner, I mean it's French AND in Black & white. It was not. It's a series of beautifully shot sequences that have relatively no narrative connection to each other or to the characters in the scenes themselves and seems to be concerned about the ennui of existence and existential angst. So you know, no tits. In effect it's like watching 472 Calvin Klein commercials in a row while melting your brain with a blow torch and replacing it with grilled Halloumi cheese.

However on Thursday nights at 6 would be the one splash of glorious vibrant in the form of one of the greatest TV shows ever made, STAR TREK!

Now whatever your opinion on Trek and it's followers it can not be denied that it's influence and storylines were groundbreaking for its time. Plus Kirk snogged Green women!

Dad and I loved it. We loved it because you always knew what you were going to get. You knew that every week Kirk would get into a ridiculous fight, McCoy would scream "I'm a Doctor Jim, not a plumber/fighter/short order cook!" This would all end up of course with an epic space battle and lots of explosions. Epic stuff.

We also loved it because my mother is an English freak. I don't mean she's a member of the EDL or anything but that she is a devout lover of the English language and abhors any kind of grammatical error. (This book has been proof read but she'll undoubtedly find the deliberate mistake I left in.)

Her problem with Star Trek is that at the beginning Kirk famously says '…to boldly go…' which is splitting an infinitive. He doesn't need to say it. So when the show started Dad or I would lean over to the TV set and turn the volume up really loud so that we could hear mother explode from the other side of the house.

"WHY DON'T THEY JUST GO! THEY COULD BE BOLD WHEN THEY GET THERE!"

This obsession with the English language and grammar also extended to diction and so my sister and I were raised listening to Radio 4 in order to promote good annunciation. A skill that I quickly dropped after the first day of secondary school. One day in a south London comprehensive and I went from having a future reading the shipping forecast to possibly appearing as a convincing street urchin in the musical 'OLIVER.'

Although this cover was blown when up to some hijinks with my new found friends I ruined the effect by shouting,

"Lordy it's the rozzers! We'll be done up like kippers unless we shift it lads."

Followed by a quick pirouette and full dance routine.

So when in 1979 'STAR TREK: THE MOTION PICTURE' came out Dad and I were ecstatic. Surely this would be the best film ever. Star Trek on the big screen would trounce that young upstart and show it who was the bigger, badder and better boss. Star Wars was a simple tale that was entertaining enough (We had seen it with Mum at the Streatham Odeon. Twice in one day as Mum fell asleep during the first showing so we stayed for the next screening. Score) but it wouldn't have any of the excitement and adventure of this young upstart.

If you have seen it then you know that it is without doubt the longest most boring film in existence and I should know, I've seen 'Last Year at Marienbad.' It goes on so long that when I went in I was 8 years old. When I came out I'd missed my first wedding.

It was such a misfire of a film. It was actually directed by the same man, Robert Wise, who had directed 'THE SOUND OF MUSIC.' Never before have I watched a Sci-Fi epic and prayed for the Von Trapp family to turn up. By half way through (roughly 6 months) there had been no fights, no exploding spaceships and more importantly no green women. It was also sad to note that he best special effect in whole film was William Shatners wig.

There were other times when we did try to have quality time together that didn't require films.

In 1983 a chap called Richard Noble broke the land speed record by driving very fast in a straight line in Nevada. In 1984 Dad won a competition to be driven around Brands Hatch race-track by Richard Noble. In a Ferrari and I was going too!

We got down to Brands Hatch, which was having a Ferrari owner's club day, which gave Dad the perfect opportunity to explain every minuscule detail of the internal combustion engine, the history of the Ferrari family & the socio-political implications of the Italian Renascence on modern day society. (When I said he knows everything, I wasn't joking.)

So we get to Brands Hatch, and are ushered into an awaiting 400i and Nobel starts the engine. He floors the accelerator and we fly down the first straight, get right to the first corner and then spin 480 degrees and end up in the barrier. Noble pulls up the handbrake, takes off his helmet and says,

"Hahahaha Terribly sorry but I'm not very good with corners!"

After that it seemed safer to stick with films.

Chapter 6

Acceptable Crying

Having an engineer for a dad would sometimes be a major bonus. Sometimes Dad would take me with him. I remember once we were in Lisbon. An amazing city, we'd spent most of the day under the stern of a ship inspecting the propeller. It was just like that scene in 'INDIANA JONES AND THE LAST CRUSADE.' You know that they are fighting by the ship with the spinning propeller? It was just like that. Exactly the same. Well the propeller wasn't spinning at all and if truth be told Dad and I weren't fighting religious zealots.

And for that matter we never found the Holy Grail but apart from all that it was exactly the same.

So that evening we have some time to kill and Dad had finished lecturing me on the historical movements of Portugals naval fleet and the success of one it's most famous navigators Vasco De Gamma so unsurprisingly we decided to go and see a movie. Lisbon is staggeringly beautiful and it's architecture dates back hundreds of years (undoubtedly helped by Portugals neutral stance in WW2) and it's cinemas are a delight. Converted theatres that still have their intricate gold embossed edging to their theatre boxes and upper circles.

When I went there seemed to be a tradition of showing films for many years. The year was 1984 and I could see massive painted billboards on top of buildings for films like '2001' and 'THE THING' in amongst new releases like 'AMADEUS', 'GHOSTBUSTERS' and 'THE ADVENTURES OF BUCKAROO BANZAI IN THE 5TH DIMENSION.' (Ok maybe not the last one but it was a real film out that year. It has Jeff Goldblum in it. Consequently it is winderfully random.)

I saw one billboard and being a young boy of 13 years of age it caught my eye. Now being 13 and interested in what all 13 year old boys who've stayed up late into the night to watch French films were interested in the image presented told me that although this was a film I needed to see, I might have a tough time persuading dad.

The image was of a girl. She was wearing hot pants, fishnet stockings, what I later learnt was called a Basque and a bowler hat. She looked hot.

As my mother had been coaching me through the power of good diction and Radio 4 I instantly worked out my strategy. I would deliver a clear ad concise speech. It would be unequivocal in it's purpose and state, nay demand, that the only course of action open to us as gentlemen travellers, and British ones at that, would be for us to proceed with all haste to yonder theatre to sample what delights it may have! I remember it clearly. One couldn't help but remember such a notable oratory delight. Forgive my indulgence but I shall relay the text of the speech word for word so that you may take solace that the future of the English language is safe.

"heydadi'mnotsureifyou'dwanttobutthere'sthatfil monoverthereitmaybegooditmaynotbutithinkiread arevueonceaboutitanditsgotgunsinitlotsofgunsand carchasesandexplosionsandprobablyfighterplanes ithinkthegirlisonlyontheppostertopromoteitwhatdo youthinkshallwegoi'msureitsreallygoodandthecar chasesaawesomeandthereslotsofexplosionsbutitco uldbeshiti'mnotsurewhatdoyouthink?"

Surely the spirit of Shakespeare looked down from the heavens and smiled knowing that the language he loved so much was in safe hands?

Now for some reason this didn't work with Dad and he wasn't too keen on showing his son 'CABARET.'

So instantly he saw a more suitable film playing in the cinema next door and so we went to see 'ESCAPE TO VICTORY.'

If you haven't seen this film then you are missing out on one of the most amazing and bizarre films ever made. For the benefit of those who haven't let me take a moment to explain the plot.

The film stars Michael Caine as a former professional footballer who is now a prisoner of war.

Max Von Sydow plays the camp commandant, a man so obsessed with football that he instantly recognises Michael Caine and organises for all the other prisoners of war who were once professional footballers to come to his camp so he can form a team.

This includes, by the way, Pele.

He then organises a match between his allied team and the German national team in the Stade de France, in Paris in the middle of occupied France.

In the meantime the Goalkeeper and mastermind of the escape plan organises for the entire team to escape during the halftime break.

It gets to half time and the Germans lead 4-1. They are about to make there escape when foolishly one of the English real life footballers is given the most important line in the film.

"Hang on, I think we can win this."

They go back.

They draw level and with seconds to spare the Goalkeeper stops a penalty that would have provided victory for the Germans.

The crowd of French civilians are ecstatic and storm the pitch gathering up our team, including Pele, and while giving them their own clothes help the entire Allied football team to escape the stadium and make their way into occupied France and to freedom.

At this point I would like to point out that the goalkeeper and therefore mastermind of the escape plan is played by Sylvester Stallone.

I'm not making this shit up people. This film REALLY happened.

Now maybe if you haven't seen the film my description may not have sold it to you. Out of 10 you may have given it a low number. Unfortunately you are wrong.

Escape to Victory is one of the most marvellously nutty films ever made. Yes it's a load of shit but it's glorious shit. By the time the allies and Pele were making their way out of the stadium I was in floods of tears and I defy anyone else not to be. The lights came up and much to my surprise I saw that my dad had shed a tear too.

This scared me to death. This man in front of me wasn't just my dad he was indestructible. He was John Wayne in British form. I had once seen my dad accidently put a nail through part of his hand, take it out with his teeth and ask me to pass the sellotape to wrap it up with. He was a God.

"Dad, have you been crying?"

'IT'S ALRIGHT SON. THERE ARE THREE OCCASIONS WHEN IT'S PERFECTLY ACCEPTABLE FOR A GROWN MAN TO CRY. THE BIRTH OF A CHILD. THE DEATH OF A LOVED ONE."

Pause.

"OR DURING A SPORTS MOVIE!"

Consequently I watch any sports movie and I'm in floods. Yes I know that our heroes will overcome adversity and become winners in the end. Yes I know that this will happen and yet I still bawl my eyes out. This goes for any sports movie too from 'THE MIGHTY DUCKS' to 'MAJOR LEAGUE', (Which in my humble opinion is the best one) I even cried at 'TIN CUP' for Christ's sake and that's about GOLF!

Of all the bizarre plot points of the film though the one I often wonder about is how does the entire Allied football team, being lead by Michael Caine, escape from occupied France?

The following sketch helps if in your head (if you're not watching it online) you do a terrible Michael Caine impersonation and a stereotypical German one. (No offense meant to Mr Caine as I am a massive fan of his work and have watched every single one of his films. Even the ones he was clearly doing to pay the rent. My favourite quote from him came when he was asked if he remembered anything about the filming of JAWS 4? "No, but I remember the house it bought." Also no offense meant to any Germans reading this as the intentional destruction of your language is done only to replicate Hollywood's inaccuracies for anything other than their own language. A fact that was made clear to me when after years of learning all the dialogue in 'DIE HARD' a German friend looked at me perplexed when I attempted a joke that involved the supposed German for 'Shoot the glass!')

EXT.   BORDER CONTROL
      DAY

Dressed in T-shirt and shorts MICHAEL CAINE approaches the control point where 2 guards are standing.

He passes over his papers.

                 GUARD 1

Comen ze here bitter?

                 MICHAEL CAINE

Yavol Herr Oberst.

                 GUARD 1

MICHAEL CAINE

Yavol Herr Oberst.

GUARD 1

MICHAEL CAINE

Yavol. Herr Oberst.

GUARD 1 returns the passport to MICHAEL CAINE

GUARD 2

Gut Luck!

MICHAEL CAINE pauses briefly then look at GUARD 2

MICHAEL CAINE

Danke.

He walks away and while he does so the guards exchange words which are subtitled as follows.

GUARD 1

Shame. I'm sure he was an escaped prisoner of war.

GUARD 2

Not with that perfect accent.

Back in Lisbon, Dads statement about crying at the birth of a child led to an obvious question about my own birth and I discovered something that I never know before.

It turns out that I was late for my own birth. They had a due date and Dad with his engineering brain had calculated everything down to the last detail and had organised to take the day in question off. However I wasn't playing by his rules and was over a month late. This was really annoying Dad (mothers response to this can not be written down for fear of the blasphemy laws) and so he engaged his engineering brain and came up with a plan to get me out of my mother.

He spent an extraordinary amount of money renting a 2 seater sports car. He then drove my mother at unrealistic speeds around Kent and he scared her so much her waters broke. He then delivered her to Beckenham hospital and after a 20 minute conversation with one of the doctors there about engine capacity (an old bedtime favourite of mine) escorted my mother to the maternity ward and was present at my birth AT 3am. I asked Dad if he cried? There was a momentary glimpse of softness in his eyes which hardened quickly as he said,

'WELL OF COURSE I DID. I WAS
SUPPOSED TO HAVE THE CAR BACK BY
FIVE. YOU COST ME A FORTUNE!"

Chapter 7

Technical Errors

One day Dad and I were supposed to go and see
'TOP GUN,' the Tom Cruise staring advert for
the American Air Force and gayest film ever
made. (If you haven't seen it check out on
YouTube Quentin Tarantino's dissection of the
film which gives a different perspective on being
someone's 'wing man.')

Accidently though we went to see 'ALIENS.'

It really was an accident as it was an 18 rated
film, I was only 15, and we took the wrong door
at the Catford ABC and found ourselves in Sci-Fi
heaven. It is a brilliant film. It also had the added
bonus that I was too young to see it legally, a fact
that my father dealt with by telling me,

"KEEP QUIET, NO ONE WILL NOTICE."

In his usually delicate tones. It didn't work
though as we were thrown out of the cinema after
half an hour because Dad had an embolism due
to his engineering brain going into meltdown.

Many a films chances of glory have been destroyed by my fathers' attention to detail. Take for example 'MASTER & COMMANDER' starring Russell Crowe, a film set on anaval boat during the reign of George the Third. Dads review was distinct.

"QUITE GOOD BUT THEY GOT A FEW THINGS WRONG!"

It's set in 1776 how does he know?

Initially however 'ALIENS' worked it's magic and impressed Dad no end with it's clever use of props.

If you've seen the film remember the big gun that the good guys have that's attached to a chest piece? Well the chest piece is actually from a steady-cam unit, the gun itself is from a Spitfire and the triggering Mechanism is actually from a Kawasaki 750R.

I know this because me dad told me so. During the film.

"OH THAT'S VERY CLEVER THEY'VE HAD TO RECYCLE IN THE FUTURE AND THAT'S WHY THAT WORKS SO WELL. WELL DONE!"

My dad thanking the cinema screen did little to placate the audience.

"Dad! Shut up you're going to get us thrown out!"

"IT'S OK SON. I'M ONLY EXPLAINING IT ALL TO THE PEOPLE."

But then something happened 27 minutes into the film (if you have the special edition 43) and Dad exploded. If you look at the scene where the troops and Ripley are walking through the laboratory for the first time, there on a table behind them for all to see, is a Tefal Deep Fat Fryer.

Oh it's there. I know this because guess who spotted it?

"WHAT IS THAT DOING THERE! THAT IS A TEFAL DEEP FAT FRYER. WHAT IS THAT DOING IN SPACE. THIS FILM IS SHIT!"

We were ejected rapidly to the delight of the other patrons.

I figure it was because of Dads attention to detail, his engineering brain couldn't justify the appearance of the fryer and it spoiled it for him. I'm not sure what was more worrying. The fact that he was prepared to let its appearance spoil his enjoyment of the film or the fact that he knew the brand?

His later thesis on the subject entitled "Why No-One in Space Fries' failed to justify his outburst despite becoming essential reading for all NASA employees.

There s only one other time when my fathers attention to detail failed him and that was at my wedding. To give you some background it should come as no doubt to you that I've had a number of different jobs in my lifetime. I've been a heating engineer, a General Manager of a garden centre and also a bouncer. No really, I was. In a gay nightclub.

I actually got the job foolishly trying to impress a young lady that worked there and as the only two straight people there, I fancied my chances.

After making my moves and charming her with the old Goatley magic (18 months of hanging around and watching from afar like a lovesick puppy I finally got to kiss her) she agreed to be my wife. The wedding was amazing, we had five drag queens, 3 transsexuals and several very nervous homophobic relatives.

The fabulous owners of the club set up the reception in the Gay nightclub. The entrance was festooned with pictures of naked men, my great Aunt Edith, who was 84 at the time (and bear in mind this was 10 years ago) still wants to go back.

Now if you have a wedding coming up or in fact any kind of celebration. May I be so bold as to suggest that you can't do any better for your entertainment purposes than having a 6ft, Glaswegian, Cher impersonator.

Just pop along to a Glasgow karaoke night and ask a 64 year old heavy set local to sing 'Turn Back Time' and you get the picture.

I still get nightmares.

Not because of the singing you understand but because while she was warbling away, Dad wandered up to me and in his usual manner told me,

'YOU KNOW THE ADVANTAGE OF SITTING AT THE BACK IS, FROM HERE, CHER LOOKS QUITE HOT!"

CHAPTER 8

Welcome to the Overlook-On-Sea

INT   MASSIVE DESERTED HOTEL
DAY

Silence fills the room as we see an enormous deserted room. It's epic size is dwarfed by the massive sweeping staircase that dominates it.

At it's base are the usual amounts of hotel furniture, sofas, chairs and tables, awaiting guests to sit there waiting for friends and family.

We move around and notice a large table at the far end. It looks as though it has been moved there. Slightly out of place. A large chair, almost throne like sits empty next to it.

On the table is an old typewriter. Reams of paper sit next to it.

We change perspective and look at the room the far end.

AIDAN dressed in a checked shirt and a corduroy dress and carrying a baseball bat enters the room.

He looks terrified.

His face seems to hold a thousand questions and all the answers look unpleasant.

He looks around keeping the bat up to him so that if anyone attacks he is ready.

He slowly, cautiously makes his way over to the table.

He approaches the typewriter.

We cannot see what he sees but instead register the confusion on his face. He rolls up the scroll and we finally see what has been written.

Row upon row it says the same thing.

ALL WORK AND NO PLAY MAKE KIMBLE A DULL DOG

AIDAN frantically looks at the ream of paper which again has the same words written in different orders all over it.

AIDANS frantic searching through the paper is suddenly stopped by a deathly howl of a hound.

Where's the scariest place you've ever seen a film? I find that unless a film is truly scary, a cinema will not bring about true fear. You're usually sitting there amongst friends with popcorn around so you know you are safe.

I once was left in the house on my own. The parents were out for the night and my sister was staying with a friend. I think I was 12. I was watching Alfred Hitchcock's 'PSYCHO' and was gripped.

After 30 minutes I'd moved the TV round so I could watch it in the relative safety of the kitchen as the patio doors in the living room could easily be breached by Norman Bates' psychotic mother.

A key scene was unfurling, the detective Arboghast was making his way upstairs towards certain doom. The tension built by the fabulous score by Bernard Hermann and the editing put the viewer on a knife-edge. He made it slowly to the top of the stairs when suddenly a door opened and…

The power went off.

A power cut.

I sat there terrified for over an hour holding a carving knife and a frying pan.

When power was restored the film has finished and I was busy turning on all of the lights in the house. My parents returned that night to find their son fast asleep in a house with the equivalent brightness of the sun armed with pots and pans in case of attack.

This was still not the scariest place I have seen a film.

That honour falls to 'THE SHINING', which I saw, in complete darkness in the middle of the North Sea.

I was 16 and Dad had got me a summer jump on a tanker ship. It was called Atlantic Superior and was owned for a Canadian shipping company and the crewmen were all Portuguese. The Captain was ex-military and wore his full uniform at all times despite now being in the merchant navy. One evening he exited his cabin to take the air wearing his pyjamas that actually had epilates and captain stripes on them.

I was planted in the medical room being an offspring of the management. The crew instantly thought I was a company spy apart from the one Brit, a Scotsman called Eddie, under who's influence I learnt the best way to swear.

There was a TV room for the officers and one for the Crew. I was allowed to use the officers room and one evening found it empty. I looked through the tapes which all seemed to be of an 'adult' nature and actually found one playing. I don't know why it had been left playing but within 30 seconds I had worked out the plot and turned it off.

So I found The Shining and put it on.

I have never been so transfixed and terrified in my entire life!

It was mesmerising and the tension was incredible. 20 minutes in the 1st mate popped his head in the door, saw me, said something in Portuguese and left.

I had never felt more alone in my entire life.

Now the corridors of an empty ship look unnervingly like a hotel and I had to walk through them to get back to my room. I slept in the TV room and again left all the lights on.

The next day despite the language barrier I could tell there seemed to be some hostility with the crew. I asked Eddie if I was imagining it and he quickly told me what was wrong.

"Some F***** put that ***ing film on last night!"

I never auditioned for RADA but if they had been there I would've got a place right there and then.

"What film?"

"the f****ing c**** Shining b******ks"

Eddie went on to explain that at the beginning of their work tour somebody had put The Shining on and the Portuguese had watched it and universally hated it. Apparently when the crew finish work and are at sea there's very little they like better than relaxing watching certain films and the VHS player in the Officers room was connected to the TV's in the cabins of the crew.

I had disturbed porn night.

Luckily armed with a Film Studies O'Level and an interpretation of the works of Kubrick put me in the perfect position to explain how this seminal film was in fact far more than it's whole & I asked Eddie if he would help me explain to the crew that this film in fact had a lot going for it and they could all enjoy it on another level.

"Don't be a prick kid. There's nae tits in it."

I had obviously not picked up my fathers ability to lecture with authority.

Chapter 9

A bit of Hollywood with Eddie

If in London, our chosen venue for a lot of films we saw together was Leicester Square the hub of the glittering West End. Situated in the heart of London this busy square with massive cinema palaces on each side was a Mecca to me as not only could you see the big Hollywood films but often you'd see someone famous either attending a premiere or just watching a film.

This led to a couple of occasions when Dad & I ran into some honest to goodness Hollywood superstars.

The first time was when Dad & I had been to see 'MIDNIGHT RUN' the excellent film starring Robert DeNiro at the Empire.

The Empire Leicester Square is an enormous cinema and tickets are about the same price as a small house so to go there was a big treat. As we exited the screen we made our way to the gents toilet and I could see there seemed to be a bit of a crowd building up.

Now remember that generational thing I was telling you about? I saw the crowd and chose to go round it to find a way into the toilets. Dad however was made of sterner stuff and obviously feeling that any impediment for a gentleman to enter a bathroom was an affront to Queen and country, he ploughed on through the crowd.

From where I know found myself directly in sight of the corridor to the gents toilet and also had a good view of my father's Trilby and umbrella battling through the crowds like Henry II at Agincourt.

I looked to the corridor and saw the biggest man I have ever seen exiting the toilets. He resembled a Zeppelin on steroids. Behind him I could make out a smaller chap, tiny in fact, and behind him another behemoth that I'm sure had a mother who loved him.

But Dad was heading right towards them.

Dad made it to the front of the corridor, the crowd had seen the Zeppelin brothers coming and obviously their small companion and got excited and a hush spread.

Then Dad got to the front of the crowd and continued down the corridor bumping into the first giant.

'EXCUSE ME.' said Dad in what I could tell was his polite voice.

He repeated the phrase with the other two and keeping his head down he proceeded to the toilets.

The effect of my fathers booming voice and his natural indignation that a gentleman should be delayed in his quest had an almost calming effect of the giants. They glanced at each other and then looked to their small friend to see if he was ok. The little man shook his head and then beamed a smile at the crowd as though nothing had happened.

The small guy was Eddie Murphy.

I went forward to the bathroom and joining father at the urinals was then stunned when a person we didn't know started to talk. (This is a truly horrifying thing when this happens as conversations in toilets for men are strictly forbidden. The average man can't cope with a chat in an elevator let alone when he is attempting to pee and has his genitalia in his hands. Needless to say there is no conversation to be had with a man trying to pee in a lift, at this point conversation would truly be dead.)

The young man, obviously excited at having seen the diminutive Mr Murphy couldn't contain himself.

"Hey, you know who that was don't ya? Eddie Murphy!"

"REALLY?" said Dad in a way that indicated that not only that he didn't care but that he may just kill if someone said another word.

"Yeah!" said the young man oblivious to his impending doom. "I wonder what he was doing here?"

Dad finishing his business as he was, zipped himself up said,

"HAVING A PISS NO DOUBT."

It was a statement of the obvious that still left the young man confused.

Chapter 10

Homo-Eroticism: With a Vengeance!

The next film on my list is Die Hard. The best action movie ever made.

It is a superb film that was made in 1989 and was the first film of the genre that took an action hero and showed he should get the absolute hell beaten out of him. Up till then we had Arnie and Stallone killing 300 plus per movie and getting a few scratches but then we got Bruce, cracking wise and getting beaten up. Sure he still killed about 300 but he broke a few ribs while doing it.

It's a very manly film. If you were going to score it oon a scale of 1 to 10 for testosterone it would score 16 and fail a drugs test. On the plus side it would win the Tour De France 7 times in a row.

It's so manly its testicles have dropped and it needs a shave before you put it in the DVD player.

I'm sure if you've seen it you'll agree with me.

It's therefore quite surprising when I tell people that 'DIE HARD' is in fact a gay love story.

Still with me?

Ok let's look at the semiotics of the film. He we have a man in a vest trapped in a situation he doesn't want to be in. A marriage that hasn't worked and is represented by the tower block that still has several layers to be finsished. Unable to come to terms with his homosexuality and a sham marriage Bruce has to fight his way out.

Outside is his lover, the cop. A man who is impotent without his lover (he is unable to fire his weapon) and it is only when Bruce accepts his homosexuality and comes 'out' of the building that he is able to once more firs his weapon and.....

Ok I know it's rubbish but this was my degree dissertation. Seriously I did a degree in Scriptwriting which means I am qualified in absolutely nothing but I can write nice stories about it.

I wrote my dissertation on 'Homoeroticism in the Action Movie' and called it 'DISSERTATION WITH A VENGEANCE!'

I wrote it purely to wind up Dad who still would have a slight heart attack at the mention of homosexuality in movies. I once mentioned the rumour that John Wayne was gay and he didn't talk to me for a week.

It's true though I did do a degree in Scriptwriting not that anything I write will ever get made. Hollywood just pretty much does remakes now. They even remade 'CLASH OF THE TITANS' an appalling remake of a classic film. It was so bad even the trailer was awful. I'm a big fan of trailers and love the way a good one is constructed. (My favourite of all time, and yes I realise how sad it is to have a favourite trailer, is for 'COMEDIAN' a Jerry Seinfeld documentary. Check it out online) Even the tagline for this film was bad. I good tagline will make a film seem exciting. I remember the tagline for 'GOLDENEYE' was 'You Know the Number!' a brilliant link into 007. The tagline for 'DIE HARD 2: DIE HARDER' was 'They said lightening never strikes twice!' Yay, same film as last time!

The tagline for 'CLASH OF THE TITANS' was this,

'TITANS WILL CLASH!'

And I've been stuck in retail for most of my life.

That may of course be that the scripts I wrote at Uni were far from popular with my tutors. For our final project the one parameter we had was that it must be a historical work. I chose to write a historical detective piece. It was called 'JESUS P.I.'

Every week our Lord Jesus Christ would solve crimes, in a mysterious way.

'What's that you say? Missing Loaves?'

"Jesus come quick, they're getting away on that boat!"

"I doubt that very much." Said Jesus as he walked across water to bring the blagards to justice.

Needless to say this didn't impress my tutors very much and I left University armed with a low degree in Scriptwriting and went out into the big wide world.

For a while I was a support worker looking after children with emotional & behavioural difficulties. Which means I spent most of my time being beaten up by 15 year olds.

Of course having a degree in Media I was soon to find my natural home, retail. For a while I was even the General Manager of a massive Garden

Centre despite knowing nothing about plants or management. Dad was very proud. I didn't have the heart to tell him I spent most of the day asking people,

"So what do you think we should do?"

And then saying something about empowerment and how we should all learn from each other. I lasted 3 years until I was found out. Garden managements gain was acting's loss.

Although I did learn very important things from my degree. If you spend 5 years watching films then you'll pick up all sorts of information like how to hack into computers, hot-wire a car and of course how to fly a plane.

There are only three things that you need to know in order to fly a plane.

1/ What the joystick does?

2/ What the pedals do?

3/ Which dial to tap when the plane runs out of fuel?

Why do they do this? Tonnes of money is thrown at these things and yet a simple tap will solve the problem?

INT.   BOMBER   PLANE
            NIGHT

The plane has been battered and bruised. The co-pilot is clearly dead and there is a fire raging in the rear of the plane. Things do not look good for our hero DAVID NIVEN as he talks to his true love of the radio.

DAVID NIVEN

Hello June. I'm terribly sorry but it doesn't look like I'm going to make it. Ginger's bought it and Tommy and Nigel are goners too. I've lost the starboard engine and the port on is in flames. Also I don't have enough fuel to climb up to clear the cliffs of Dover. Afraid I'm going to have to bail out.

JUNE(OS)

Oh my darling I'm sure you'll survive.

DAVID NIVEN

Problem is dear that my parachute went up in flames over Bordeaux. I'm sorry dear but this really will be it my darling.

PAUSE

JUNE(OS)

Darling, have you tried taping the fuel gauge?

DAVID NIVEN

Oh crikey no completely forgot.

DAVID NIVEN taps on the fuel gauge and the starboard engine springs to life.

He taps again and the co-pilot shakes his head awake and give him the thumbs up.

                    DAVID NIVEN

        It's worked darling!

(I would like to point out that my university has produced many top quality people in their chosen fields while I spent far too much time having fun and playing Playstation games with my fellow layabouts. One friend from Uni recently had lunch with Jack Nicholson in Jack Nicholson's house interviewing him because he's now one of the editors of the biggest & best film magazines.

As I write this I'm sitting in Brighton Library with half a coffee and an empty snickers wrapper by my side and wondering whether I can claim that the tramp sitting to my left is just Robert DeNiro researching his next role. He isn't. I just asked)

Chapter 11

The Worst Film Ever Made

Life moves on and after University it kind of got in the way (Dear Jen I mean in a massively positive way my darling xxx) of Dad & I going to the cinema. So it was quite a while until we got a chance to get to the cinema again and it was to see what can only be described as the worst film ever made. Avatar.

Yes I'm aware that it made more money than God and it was nominated for 642 Oscars but it is an appalling film and for those that haven't seen it yet I will tell you how to avoid the horrors of watching this horrible tosh.

First go to the shops and buy a tin of Quality Street.

Go home and remove the blue ones.

Take the wrappers and place them over your eyes.

And then just watch 'DANCES WITH WOLVES!'

It is the same film. They should have just called it Dances with Smurfs it's so similar. Its main message is that machines are bad and trees are good.

That's it really. Machines are bad and Trees are good.

FOR THREE HOURS!

I sat there in absolute fury as this dire mess of a movie unfolded and couldn't believe how enraptured people had been of it. I was however sure of one thing, Dad would be hating it too. Remember when I said that Dad know everything there is to know about everything? I wasn't joking, he really does. He has three degrees in total.

One in Advanced Engineering, one in Advanced Mathematics and one in Chemisty.

This means he knows exactly how something has gone wrong, how to fix it and also time travel.

So I was pretty sure I'd know Dads reaction to this nonsense. To give you an idea of how silly this film is, sorry this Oscar nominated film, specifically Best 'ORIGINAL' screenplay film is I should tell you briefly about it.

Humans and machines are bad, trees and blue aliens are good (although they do need to be saved by the white man hero which of course brings up a whole other debate) and humans are after a mineral that is only available on the blue peoples planet.

The name of the mineral in this OSCAR NOMINATED script (and bear in mind I have a degree in scriptwriting and work currently in a pet store) is amazing called UNOBTAINIUM!

Seriously.

Unobtainium.

I have never been more angry in my entire life.

How the hell did this get made let alone praised enough to get an Oscar nominaton?

The only things stopping me from exploding there and then was the safe knowledge that Dad would be exploding too. After all this was the man that got us thrown out of Aliens because of a deep fat fryer. Unobtainium would surely be making him explode like Krakatoa!

"I THOUGHT IT WAS BRILLIANT!"

"WHAT!"

I exploded with rage. How was this possible? This was a man who had lived his life and ruled mine by a set of parameters that were set in stone. It was a simple code and everything just followed suit. It was the natural way of things, everyone knew that you always wore matching colour belt and shoes, you never had ketchup with a steak and any massive inconsistency in a film rendered it pointless.

I was astounded. If I could I would have given him a lecture, produced a copy of the periodic table and asked him where! Where on this table (the very tool he had lived his life by) was UNOBTAINIUM?

His reply?

'IT'S ONLY A MOVIE SON'

I couldn't let that go. I just couldn't. So for the benefit of the show and my sanity I got on the phone and tried to get Dad to come down and talk about AVATAR.

INSERT KIMBLE CLIP HERE

(Apologies for not writing a description of the final clip but it really does have to be seen to be believed but it does end up with Kimble wearing 3D glasses & watching the film)

So Dad didn't make it that day. He has since seen the previous clip with Kimble and his reaction was just like the Dad of old."

"YOU DO REALISE THAT YOUR DOG IS COLOUR BLIND?"

I don't think Dad was prepared to admit defeat with regards to that film. You see he may have mellowed slightly over the years but he has always been incredibly competitive and I think he realised I'd won about AVATAR.

So his saying 'It's only a movie" was his way of winning, of not admitting defeat.

At that point I realised that I've never beaten him at anything. It's stupid I know but the John Wayne mentality that I'd been brought up with took over and I became determined to beat him at something, if only to have a finale for my show.

The amazing thing is that he's so bloody good at so many things I was going to have trouble beating him to anything.

It was then I had what alcoholics call a moment of clarity. If I did something he's never done before then surely I would have won. The very fact that he'd never given it a go would mean that I would win no matter what.

Genius Right?

So it became clear what I should do. I knew that Dad had never done any running so if I did a race it wouldn't matter where I came because I would still be better. That idiotic macho need to better my father got in the way of any logic. So I entered the Brighton Marathon.

Stupid Right?

Just in case you're wondering the Brighton marathon is still 26 miles. Just because it's in Brighton doesn't mean we get time off for wearing the Vegas showgirl outfits.

It is without doubt the stupidest thing I have ever done in my life. (And I once watched 'ISHTAR' of my own free will and liked it.)

I did no training whatsoever apart from buy a proper pair of trainers and do a 5K run with zero preparation. The 5K I managed to do in an appalling time of 32 minutes and managed to beat a 74 year old woman in the final straight. I say beat, I actually kicked her to the ground with 20 metres to go but a win is a win right?

So the day of the marathon was here and following age old advice from my father in any endeavour I stood right at the back of the crowd.

My thinking being that if I started last, it could only get better. How wrong I was as.

I was in so much pain my hips had declared war on the rest of my body and were in danger of winning.

But I still couldn't give up. The John Wayne Macho gene was still kicking in and I had to prove a point. I vowed to make it to the finish and 9hours and 46 minutes after starting I virtually crawled to the end.

One of the attendants shouted encouragement as I waddled by,

"Get to the end mate, the announcer will call your name and the crowd is still there!"

Brighton is an amazing city and I have never been more pleased to be a resident of it when I looked up to see hundreds of people still out and cheering the last of the latecomers as the announcer called out names.

It was then that I spotted him.

There amongst the crowd and surrounded by a bunch of guys I later learnt were the Brighton Gay Mens Chorus was my Dad. He had come to cheer me on and he had stayed to the bitter end.

It was then I knew my moment had come. This was the time I would finally win. I would finally get one up on this man. The man who was my hero, the living embodiment of John Wayne.

I picked up my pace to at least 1 mile an hour and heard the announcer call,

"AND COMING UP HERE WE CAN SEE AN AMAZING SIGHT..."

This was it. I was ready to win.

Unfortunately I didn't realise one important fact. In my quest for stupid glory I didn't realise at first that the announcer was not calling out for me but for a group of three Japanese students behind me. They had constructed and carried a

20ft replica of the Bullet Train around the 26 miles for a Tsunami relief charity.

And they overtook me.

They got to the finish line and everyone went mental. The crowds, the announcer and also the Gay Mens Choir but not Dad. He stood there and waited for me to finish.

It was then I realised how stupid I had been. I mean I'm a grown man and here I was carrying on like some 15 year old desperate for attention, trying to win against a man who was only trying to find the best way to communicate with me.

I went over to him,

"Well Dad. What d'you think?"

"I THOUGHT IT WAS A DISGRACE!"

A bit harsh I thought.

Dad pointed to the Japanese train.

"THEY CLEARLY HAD AN AERODYNAMIC ADVANTAGE!"

Chapter 12

The best movie ever made

We come to the last film of the show.

(Not of Dad & I as thankfully we still have been able to attend the cinema together. When I was a young boy I got into reading comics and specifically 2000ad so it was with great pleasure we went to see the film 'DREDD' recently)

THE BLUES BROTHERS is in my mind the best film ever made and is my absolute favourite. It came out in the early eighties and didn't set the box office alight but by mid-decade it had become a cult classic and was being shown every Friday at the Baker Street Odeon. Dad took me to see it as he had heard how good a film it was.

It was awesome. It was a musical, a comedy, and it had car chases and an array of cameos like I had never seen. James Brown, Aretha Franklin & Ray Charles to name but a few. It blew me away, not just the film but the music too. I had never been exposed to this music before and afterwards I discovered that this was Dads favourite type of music. He, of course, knew everything about it and we spent the journey home talking about the Blues from Robert Johnson to BB King.

It was great to be talking about something together. Sure it had started with films but it was a different subject for us.

We got home and Dad said,

"WELL SEEING AS HOW YOU SEEM TO LIKE THE BLUES SO MUCH. NEXT YEAR AS A TREAT, WHY DON'T WE GO TO CHICAGO AND LISTEN TO SOME BLUES!"

Wow. That would be incredible. So this was in 1986.

In 2001 we finally went.

That's my dad there standing with my identical thinner cousin. (it was over 10 years ago and my diet starts tomorrow. Honest)

This was the car he rented, a red Ford Mustang convertible. We were going on a road trip from Washington to Indianapolis to watch the Formula 1 Grand Prix. The blues was still with us both but our aim was to stop briefly in Chicago on the way.

The trip was eventful to say the least with dads specific itinerary we had a lot of miles to cover and God help us if we stayed in one place longer than 8 hours.

We unfortunately got lost at one point in Baltimore.

In the Hood.

For those of you unaware of the delights of Baltimore and if you haven't seen 'THE WIRE,' imagine the worst parts of hell and add automatic weapons.

My fathers instant response was to stop and ask for directions.

"FROM THOSE YOUNG CHAPS OVER THERE!"

Believe me when I say this was the first and undoubtedly the last time a Baltimore street gang was referred to as 'Chaps.'

I needn't of worried though as we did indeed get the directions we needed from the chaps (who were fine once they realised we were English and not any threat) with the added bonus of some crack. From a lovely chap called 'Blood.'

As we drove away we were both relieved that all was ok and I laugh now about Dads putting on the central locking on a convertible car.

So we made it to Chicago and as we had the luxury of a whole day till we moved on we decided to tour Chicago and it's movie locations.

Chicago is a magnificent city and as full and vibrant as you'd imagine it to be. It's located right next to Lake Michigan (If you're British forget any concept you may have of a lake in your head. This is a sea in anyone else's mind) so you have the wonderful sight of skyscrapers next to a beach.

We went to Union station so we could see the stairs where 'THE UNTOUCABLES' has its 'BATTLESHIP POTEMPKIN' inspired shoot out. It was quite something to stand mid-way on the steps, as commuters happily walked up the other side, while Dad took a picture of me pretending to be Kevin Costner reaching for the pram that was heading for doom at the bottom.

INSERT PICTURE

Dad then made me take a picture of him pretending to be Robert DeNiro despite my assurances that as DeNiro does not appear in that scene he'd have to pretend to be someone else. Dad then gave me a look that indicated that as he was paying for this trip that if he wanted to be DeNiro pulling a gun on the steps then he would be DeNiro pulling a gun on the steps.

We then went on the El train. I tried to get Dad to run underneath it pretending to be Gene Hackman in 'THE FRENCH CONNECTION' but he wasn't having any of it.

So that evening we're in town and looking for a film to watch when Dad remembered his promise and said we should go and find some blues somewhere.

So we ended up in a place called 'The House of Blues' a massively cool blues venue which is owned by Dan Ackroyd, one of the stars of The Blues Brothers.

Needless to say this was the coolest evening ever. There I was with my Dad, in Chicago, watching a Blues player twanging away. How much cooler could this be?

The guy on stage was exceptionally cool and held the audience as he sang and played his heart out.

This couldn't get any better.

And then amazingly it did.

The player left the stage and the announcer came on.

"We're gonna have a little break now of 5 or 10 minutes but don't go anywhere because we have a special treat after... The Blues Brothers Band!"

Oh.

My.

God.

The crowd went absolutely nuts as did I. How amazing was this? What were the chances of this happening on the very day that Dad & I were there?

I turned to Dad and laughed and acted like a 5 year old. Wow this was just outstanding.

And that's when he told me that we weren't going to the Grand Prix. We never were. We were always coming to the House of Blues. You see the reason we didn't go in 1987 was that Dad couldn't afford it.

He had a dream of taking his son on an amazing road trip across America in a car. Not just any car as it had to be a Ford Mustang convertible, a red one. So that he and his on could wear sunglasses and look cool as we travelled to the home of his favourite music. So he spent the next 15 years saving the money to make his dream trip so that we could do the trip in the style he wanted to do it in. It was only when he found out that The Blues Brothers Band were reforming just for a special night that he knew this was now the time for us to go.

When he told me I was just blown away. To think that for 15 years he had kept this plan secret was just incredible. I didn't know how to react I wanted to hug him and tell him how my heart was bursting with love for him. How it always had and that I loved him.

But of course I couldn't because of the macho John Wayne bullshit that I'd been filled with since childhood.

So all I could do was turn to him and say,

'THIS IS GREAT!"

And Dad turned to me. Took off his sunglasses and with tears in his eyes and in the softest tone I've ever heard him speak said,

"And I love you too."

That is the end of my story. I guess the moral if you want one is if there's someone you haven't seen in a while, it could be your mum or dad, 2nd cousin or just an old friend. Give them a call & maybe catch a movie together.

You don't have to tell them you love them but it's always nice to be reminded.

Take care.

X

INSERT END TITLES

The Riddle of the Pavilion

"We are men of honour Herr Winchester." Said Von Steghiem "Surely as such these matters can not be concluded with these piffling tools of war?"
Winchester loosened his grip on the pistol and threw it to the ground.

"What would you suggest Count?" he replied, fully aware that Colonel Juniper would have the devil in his sights by now.

"Why sabre's of course dear boy. Is that not how you Englishmen 'prove your metal as such?"

Lord Winchester smiled, bowed his head and was unsurprised to see his nemesis flicking his wrist, resulting in a smaller pistol, a Derringer, in his hand

"Well that's far from sporting old chap."

"Indeed Herr Winchester but I'm quite bored of our confrontations."

"Me too" said Winchester with a knowing smile. The blagard raised his pistol and then suddenly a shot rang out in the distance and struck him square in the chest sending him sprawling back 3 foot.

"Not today Count. Not today."

Lord Winchester looked up to the far hill and gave the signal to his sharp-shooting comrade in arms. Colonel Juniper responded by standing up and making his way down to the site of Count Wilfred Von Steighiem's recent demise.

Winchester knelt down next to the corpse and removed the papers that had been secreted in his jacket pocket.

Interesting." said his Lordship, his stern blue eyes looking across the manifest. "It would seem that the museum delivery was signed for by our recently departed Mr Harrow!"

"But... But he's been dead for nearly 2 days!" said Colonel Juniper arriving at his side.
"Exactly" said Lord Winchester, momentarily distracted by the signature at the bottom of the page. "Remind you of anything, old chap?"
The Colonel squinted at the document and then gasped as he recognised the penmanship.
"Good God your Lordship. Cairo!"
Both men had barely made it out of Egypt following their recent adventure in Africa, but they both knew that trouble was coming their way.

Trouble, that, until then had never dared rear it's head on British soil!

"Never be embarrassed dad. Embarrassment is how we learn to live."

"Wow. That's quite profound Rosie."

"I know. It was on Cartoon Network."

- Rosie Goatley 2015

That's it.

L - #0063 - 150219 - CO - 210/148/11 - PB - DID2445642